The Making of A Well-Designed Business®

LuAnn Nigara

Published by Best Seller Publishing®, Pasadena, CA
Best Seller Publishing® is a registered trademark
Printed in the United States of America.
ISBN: 978-1-946978-54-7

This publication is designed to provide accurate and authoritative information with regard to the subject matter covered. It is sold with the understanding that the publisher is not engaged in rendering legal, accounting, or other professional advice. If legal advice or other expert assistance is required, the services of a competent professional should be sought. The opinions expressed by the authors in this book are not endorsed by Best Seller Publishing® and are the sole responsibility of the author rendering the opinion.

Most Best Seller Publishing® titles are available at special quantity discounts for bulk purchases for sales promotions, premiums, fundraising, and educational use. Special versions or book excerpts can also be created to fit specific needs.

For more information, please write:
Best Seller Publishing®
1346 Walnut Street, #205
Pasadena, CA 91106
or call 1(626) 765 9750
Toll Free: 1(844) 850-3500
Visit us online at: www.BestSellerPublishing.org

This book was a blast to write, and it is, without doubt, a culmination of so many loving and talented people who have taught and influenced me throughout my life. However, there are three people, in particular, I want to acknowledge and thank with my whole heart.

Thank you, Mom. Thank you for always saying to me "You can do it."

Thank you, Dad. Thank you for always saying to me "Why do you think you can do it?"

Thank you, Al. Being a stepparent is the most delicate of relationships, and your quiet support is always noticed and valued.

I love all of you tons. It is truly because of you, my parents, that I have every mental and emotional skill I need to succeed.

Testimonials

"LuAnn is succinct, comprehensive, intuitive, and REAL! She gets down to the basics – with excellent tips for systems, inspirational anecdotes, and a reality check reminding us that hard work and knowing who you are is what it takes to create a business that is well designed for YOU! If you have questions about the interior design business, listen to LuAnn's podcast – A Well-Designed Business – she is relentless at getting the answers I want to know each and every time with a terrific sense of humor and unsurpassed integrity."

– Debra Phillips

"Reading The Making of A Well-Designed Business is like having your best friend sitting next to you on your comfy sofa, giving you the best business advice possible. LuAnn is real, she's approachable, she's encouraging, plus she really wants you to succeed. The business insight she shares in the book comes from years of experience and believe me she knows her stuff! But as great as that is, her desire to helps others succeed in business is what takes this book to a deeper level."

– Beth Clarkson

"A friend of mine this year introduced me to LuAnn's podcast "A Well-Designed Business", and I've been following her work since. When this book came out, I knew I had to get it. As a solopreneur and starting my business, this book was so helpful to me. It gave me such great value and insight of what steps to take as you start, how to structure your business and the importance of doing it from the very beginning. It highlights real life experiences and examples, which is great. This book is good for anyone that has a business or wants to start one. I highly recommend."

– Mari Gon

"I have been listening to LuAnn's podcast, A Well-Designed Business for two years and it has been instrumental in helping me to start my business. And now a book? What?! Get out! I love it! It's concise and hit on all the important stuff. No meaningless fluff or yah yah nonsense, it's all gold. Follow the guidelines in this book and you will be a success! I highly recommend it!"

— Wingnut McGeeon

"This book is a must-have read for small business owners — not just those within the interior design field. It's succinct, actionable, and easy to digest. As a new business owner, we can be flooded with information and what LuAnn has done in this book is provide you with a high level, actionable roadmap to help guide you to success, and spur you into action. As a regular podcast listener, I believe she truly has a gift for pulling out the golden nuggets from each guest interview and translating that into clear action for her listeners. She's done that here in this book for her readers as well. Very happy I purchased!

- Thanh Buswell

"I thoroughly enjoyed this valuable business book! The Making of A Well-Designed Business is not only perfect for anyone starting a business, it is equally as valuable to those looking to reboot an existing business. LuAnn beautifully outlines the foundations of running a profitable business in a way that makes it simple to understand and highly implementable. The discussion about creating successful systems, hiring your "Dream Team", and making customer satisfaction a priority is just part of the amazing business advice that will contribute to your business profitability and success. It's a must read. Thanks LuAnn, as a business coach to creative entrepreneurs, I will be making this required reading!"

— Nang

"LuAnn came to me via her podcast well into her 2nd year of doing that. I follow her on Facebook and have met her offline, as I say now. When she told us about her new book, I knew I would immediately want to read the

words of wisdom from this go-getter. After all, she runs a very successful business AND a very successful podcast for the interior design world (though many could get hints from people she interviews).

The book does a great way at teaching you a pathway to success, while recognizing that you can get in the way of this, and her chapter about client retention is pretty on target. In my industry, clients are always right, isn't always so, we don't take clients who are difficult. This leaves room for taking the 80% of clients who aren't. There is that 80/20 rule working that LuAnn mentions in her book.

If you want to learn the important thing about running a well-designed business in 94 pages, and are willing to put the work in, this book is for YOU!"

– H. BATESON

"As someone who ran a national sales/service organization, I found that The Making of A Well-Designed Business would be extremely valuable as a tool for companies with remote offices which have to operate somewhat independently while maintaining corporate missions and identities. The book is concise and pleasantly readable. Its like being personally coached as opposed to reading a text. I highly recommend this book for individual entrepreneurs and corporate personnel."

– ROBERT OBRIEN

Table of Contents

Introduction

Being self-employed was supposed to set you free, wasn't it? You probably love what you do, so you started your business with dreams of financial freedom. Instead, are you working twelve- to fourteen-hour days, earning little or no money, wondering what went wrong?

You picked up this book because you want to know what makes a business successful—what makes it profitable. Maybe you are looking for the magic pill, the new idea, the "aha" moment, to unlock the mysteries of what and how to be successful.

Good news, this book is for you.

I'm going to walk you through step-by-step what it takes to create or to recreate a business that is well run and profitable and gives you the income and lifestyle you imagined for yourself.

But first, should we just start here on page one with the secret to success? Do you want the magic pill? Okay, I'll spill the beans right up front rather than waiting until the last chapter. This way, you'll know if this book is for you before you go any further. And if you stay with me after this introduction, I'll also know you're my kind of entrepreneur.

Let me explain the secret to your business success—your magic pill.

When I started ninth grade, my parents taught me a lesson that laid the foundation for every success I've enjoyed since.

I went to a parochial grammar school, and when I graduated, only six or eight of my classmates went with me to the public high school; the rest went to the Catholic high school.

It was the first week of high school, and I was just like a kid in a candy shop! There were ski clubs, Spanish clubs, choirs, sports, and student government. And next to the sports, student government was the one that got my attention because, well, in full disclosure, I was going to be president of the United States (POTUS) someday, so this was clearly my stepping-stone, right?

So, what in the world was student government? I had no idea, but in one week, the freshman class was going to gather in the cafeteria and cast their votes for the freshman class student board. Wahoo, this was for me! After school, I announced to both of my parents, "I am running for vice president of the freshman class."

"What is that?" my mother asked immediately.

"I have no idea, but that's exactly why I'm running for VP. I figure I'll be involved for a year and find out how to do it, and then next year, I'll run for president."

She turned and said, "What makes you think anyone else knows how to do it? You should run for president."

When I started to speak, my dad jumped in, raised his voice, which he rarely did, and told my mother, "Stop filling her head with dreams. Don't encourage her! She'll never get elected VP or president or anything else on that board!"

As I was about to ask why the heck not, what's wrong with me, my mom jumped on him. It was the kind of moment when the argument just went to an adult level, and I as the kid had better shut up. She snapped back at him saying, "She can do anything she wants to do. Don't you dare tell her she can't do something."

My dad went on, talking about how it wasn't a matter of what I wanted to do. Then he looked at me and asked, "Do you know who is running for president?" After I told him, he looked at us and said,

"See, that girl is from this school. There are 120 kids in the class, and you know a half dozen of them; she knows everyone else. You have no chance at all of winning this election in one week."

You see my dad was a businessman himself. He had been self-employed his entire life, and he knew no matter how wonderful my mom was to believe in me—to believe in all of us—success wasn't something you just wished for. He was a hard worker, and he was an even smarter man. Over the years, he ran several businesses. He owned a diner, a pizza shop, and a taxi business, and he ran Holiday Lake. Holiday Lake was a resort in South Jersey that, from the late '50s through the '70s, was the area's best family summertime spot. People came from all over South Jersey and Philadelphia to go to Holiday Lake. There was swimming, picnicking, tennis, boat rides, mini golf, you name it. My dad first worked for his parents there, and then my parents took over after them. My dad ran the entire enterprise for nearly twenty-five years. Dozens of my cousins (I have about fifty cousins) worked for my dad there in their teens; it was like a rite of passage in the Schwartz family. To this day, my cousins speak highly of my dad and of their stint working for him at Holiday Lake. It is common for me to hear "How is your dad doing? I just love Uncle Don. Working for him at the Lake was one of my best experiences ever." My dad always had the right mix of getting the work done and having a great time doing it. Always ready to crack a joke and make everyone feel great. He influenced many of us by his example.

While my parents continued to debate, I thought about my dad's point. He made a good one. So what was I to do? Wait another year until I knew all or most of the kids?

No way.

I made a decision.

And I needed a plan.

So the next day, with my goal in mind and my plan all set, I went to school. I asked every person I crossed paths with, are you in the freshman class? Are you in the freshman class? Do you know someone in the freshman class? It was like the Dr. Seuss book, *Are You My Mother?* Every time I heard yes, I would say, "My name is LuAnn Schwartz, and I'm running for class president. I know you don't know me, but I promise you I will do my very best to lead this class if you vote for me for president. I will do a great job."

I did this every day for a week; I was the geekiest, nerdiest kid in our class. But one week later, I was the happiest girl in the world when I walked into our kitchen and told my parents I was voted president of the freshman class. I remained president for four years.

Sadly, however, I never became POTUS.

What's the moral of the story?

It's the magic pill.

You need to be a little like my mother, with unwavering confidence in yourself, in your product, in your service. And then you need to be like my dad, with eyes wide open, facing the obstacles, looking out for the pitfalls. And then you need to be like me, make a plan, a detailed roadmap to achieve your goals. Think about it, confidence and goals without a plan won't get you anywhere, but a plan and goals without confidence won't work either. You need all three.

And then you need to decide.

Decide to be excellent because, make no mistake about it, excellence is a decision. Excellence in business, heck, excellence in doing anything and everything can only happen if and when you decide you will do your very best and nothing less.

Decide to do what it takes to be successful. It may not be easy, it may not be comfortable, but if you are to succeed and have a profitable business, it always starts with a decision—a decision to execute.

I share this book with my husband, Vin Nigara, and our cousin Bill Campesi. I'm the one with the pen to paper, but for certain, it's together that the three of us have earned the lessons contained here on how to run a successful business.

We decide every day to be excellent.

In addition to our commitment to our business, our employees, and, most importantly, our customers, serendipity played a small role. We came together in the early '80s to launch Window Works because of our personal connections. Little did we know how perfectly suited we were to be business partners. Have you read the *E-Myth* by Michael Gerber? (If you haven't, promise me it will be the next business book you read after this one). Michael Gerber explains that to be successful, every business owner needs to be part Technician, part Manager, and part Entrepreneur. We are so at blessed at Window Works because while each of us have skills that overlap the three ideals, we each have an individual "superpower" that aligns exactly with the criteria for success according to Michael Gerber. Bill is the Technician; he is quite literally one of the most knowledgeable and talented window treatment installers in the business. My husband, Vin, is the Manager, keeping us financially sound, monitoring our day-to-day operation, and ensuring our profitability. And then there is me, the Entrepreneur, the dreamer, the one who works *on* our business not just *in* our business, the one who looks to the new next thing, like this book and our podcast, *A Well-Designed Business®*, found on iTunes, Stitcher, and iHeartRadio. Together we have created a business we are tremendously grateful for and proud of.

While we too are always on the lookout for the next idea, the next thing that will make us at Window Works magically more prosperous, we have had successes these last thirty plus years. In addition to the three of us, we have six employees. In 2016, we grossed more than $2 million in sales, with three of us in the sales role. And, back in the day, from the late '70s through the early '90s, Window Works was a franchise, with over ninety operating Window Works showrooms across the United States. We owned three locations, opening our first location in 1982 and our second and third locations in 1984. The franchise disbanded in 1994 but from 1984 to 1994 our three locations earned highest gross sales, first, second and third place every single year. Over these last thirty plus years, we have contracted and serviced more than 24,000 customers for window treatments and awnings.

I know if you decide to follow the lessons that Vin, Bill, and I have learned, you too will have a business that is successful and profitable and that you will be proud of just as we are of ours.

So let's get you on the path to making your own well-designed business.

CHAPTER 1

Establish Your Company Mission and Core Values

One of the first things I want to impress upon you, whether you are a new business owner or have been in business many years, is you must take the time to establish your mission statement and your core values. I learned this from my husband, Vin. He was quite clear and direct about the need for it to be established, to be enunciated, and also the need for it to be basic and straightforward. For Window Works, he said our mission is to be the very best at filtering light and providing privacy at the window. He said that to do this and to do it better than anyone else is our main objective every day.

Vin explained knowing your mission gives you clarity, especially when you are a new business. So, for example, when you consider adding a product or service, you ask yourself, does it support your company mission? A good question to ask yourself whenever you are doing anything is, why? Why are you doing this? What do you hope to accomplish? Does it align with your company mission, and does it serve your company core values? In our case, after opening, Vin decided to add awnings to our product mix, and later he decided to add window tinting. Both support our mission. But when I wanted to add accessories and furniture to our showroom, he said, "No, ma'am. They don't support our mission, and anything that doesn't support our mission potentially distracts us." *Ixnay on furniture*. Good decision.

Another important conversation to have with yourself is about your company core values. At Window Works, our core values are integrity and 100 percent customer satisfaction. My father-in-law was instrumental in our developing these values.

One evening, we were having dinner at my parents-in-law's, and I had been in the family about a year at the time. While my mother-in-law was putting dinner on the table, my father-in-law came through the back door from work. He went over to the sink to wash his hands and began talking about his day and how one of his customers had been unhappy. He was going to have to redo something, which would cost him money he hadn't budgeted in the price of the project.

As he was describing what had happened, my brother-in-law said, "Well, Dad, why don't you just tell the customer that you can't do it?"

My father-in-law looked over at him, at all of us, and said, "What do mean, son?"

"Well, just explain that you hadn't counted on that being a part of the job and that you have to bill more money because it wasn't your fault."

Then my father-in-law looked at his son and said, "I'm not going to do that, and you know why? Because my name is Anthony Nigara, and I gave the customer a quote for the job, and I'm not going to raise that price because another tradesperson made a mistake. I gave her my word. My word is my name, and my name is Nigara. That means something to me, and I hope it means something to you too. Your name says to everyone who you are."

I was stunned and excited. It was like listening to Tony Robbins. We were running Window Works at that point, and I thought, "Well, that's how I want it to be in our business; I want to make sure that when I give my word to my customers, they can trust that I will follow through with it."

8

My father-in-law's words weren't just some lip service he told all of us. It was what he truly believed. He wasn't just talking the talk; he walked the walk. He was born in 1912 and was of what is called the Greatest Generation—the men and women who fought in World War II. That was exactly who my father-in-law was. He was a proud and principled man. He was a master plumber and owner of his own business for more than sixty years, and he was well respected and beloved in the community.

Through Window Works, I have had the opportunity to meet a lot of people in our community. When I married my husband and took the Nigara name, people often asked if I was related to Tony Nigara. When I told them he was my father-in-law, they would say, "That man is a gentleman. He has done our plumbing for decades," or "He does my mother's plumbing. What a kind man, always there when you need him, always sticks to the work, always stands behind his work." Everywhere I went in town, he was well-known and respected. It was clear that he had run his business all those years exactly the way he said.

I wanted our business to have the same kind of reputation and to handle our relationships with our clients the same way my father-in-law had. And that is exactly what we have done. We have adopted the two core values, integrity and 100 percent customer satisfaction. His example has greatly affected Window Works and contributed to our company's fantastic growth.

Why It Matters

When you as the owner of your business first decide what your core values are and then exemplify them to your employees, it makes it so much easier for your employees to handle their day. It gives them a protocol for when problems arise, which creates an environment where they all can be comfortable in their jobs. They know they can handle situations with customers and vendors on your behalf because they know what your most important criteria are in all situations.

In our case, our team is clear on our values. Under no circumstances will we compromise our integrity or our commitment to serving our customers' best interest. These are nonnegotiable. Because of this, all problems can be handled without anxiety about the unknown, about the process. We don't pass responsibility off to our customers. We don't blame our customers because they didn't read our contract or because they didn't tell us something that we should have asked.

Here is a perfect example of our team working in unison within our core values.

I had a large shutter project in South Orange. I met with the customer and measured the windows. Then we selected all the details, I wrote the order, and the customer gave me the deposit.

Six weeks later, my partner Bill left in the morning to install the shutters, but when I saw him coming back about an hour later, I thought, uh oh, that's not good.

As it turned out, this house had all tilt-in windows, the kind you clean from the inside. Bill explained to me if he had installed the style shutter I had ordered, the customer wouldn't be able to tilt her windows in for cleaning. Yikes! I had missed that; I had completely missed it. Holy moly, a $15,000 job that was now firewood!

What happened next?

My partner Bill had been on the front line with that customer, and he didn't dance, he didn't wonder if he needed to speak with Vin or with me before offering solutions that would cost us money. No, because he knew our priority was not our net profit on a project but 100 percent customer satisfaction, he was free to simply and humbly say to our customer: "I am very sorry. LuAnn has made a mistake. While you may not have noticed it for many months, I can see it now. I'm sorry; however, I do have a solution I'd like to explain it to you."

We didn't count dollars in making it right; we didn't ask our customer to pay for it, or even part of it because she didn't say anything about her tilt-in windows. We made it right; it ate into our profits, and that's how it went.

But when we finished, our customer was so pleased with our honesty, our professionalism, and the outcome that she ordered shutters for four more rooms.

We decide to work with integrity and to provide excellent customer service every time, not just when it's easy or when it's free.

In a way, opening a business is like having a baby. Before you have the baby, you take the time to think about what it means to you and to your family. You have long discussions with your partner about your ideals, what kind of parents you will be, and what values you will have for your child. This way when things get sticky, you can go back and say, we decided this, or we agreed to that. It is exactly the same when you take the same time to decide your company mission, your company core values, and what kind of reputation you want when you start your business. Can you see how it makes it easier in the day to day and in crisis to do the right thing simply and easily?

Start by understanding this simple truth: You are in charge of your business. And if you don't want to see it fizzle out like so many others, you need to make good decisions now. Decisions that will enable you to build a business that two, three, or four decades from now is something with your name on it that you have run well and something you are proud of.

Take a minute now to think about what matters most to you as the owner of your business, as the leader of your company.

What is your company mission?

What are your core values?

To help you brainstorm, consider the mission statements and core values of Infusionsoft and SquareSpace.

Infusionsoft's mission is to "help small businesses thrive with sales and marketing software built for them."[1] Their values are as follows:

- We empower entrepreneurs.
- We listen, we care, we serve.
- We do what we say we'll do.
- We practice open, real communication.
- We face challenges with optimism.
- We check our egos at the door.
- We innovate and constantly improve.
- We do the right thing.
- We believe in people and their dreams.[2]

SquareSpace's mission is "Giving voice to ideas."[3] They have the following values:

- Be your own customer
- Empower individuals
- Design is not a luxury
- Good work takes time
- Optimize toward ideals
- Simplify.[4]

1   Y Scouts (2015, May 15). Top 10 Core Values At The Top 10 Medium Sized Workplaces [Web log post]. Retrieved November 28, 2017, from https://yscouts.com/culture-2/top-10-core-values-medium-workplaces/

2   Y Scouts (2015, May 15). Top 10 Core Values At The Top 10 Medium Sized Workplaces [Web log post]. Retrieved November 28, 2017, from https://yscouts.com/culture-2/top-10-core-values-medium-workplaces/

3   Y Scouts (2015, May 15). Top 10 Core Values At The Top 10 Medium Sized Workplaces [Web log post]. Retrieved November 28, 2017, from https://yscouts.com/culture-2/top-10-core-values-medium-workplaces/

4   Y Scouts (2015, May 15). Top 10 Core Values At The Top 10 Medium Sized Workplaces [Web log post]. Retrieved November 28, 2017, from https://yscouts.com/culture-2/top-10-core-values-medium-workplaces/

CHAPTER 2

Your Dream Team

Before you open your doors, before you get your business cards, and before you set up your website, you need to assemble your team of experts and mentors. These are the people you will rely on throughout your business career for sound, objective advice.

The Nonnegotiable Experts

Trusted mentor. Even the savviest person is well served by having a business mentor, someone who has more business experience than you. Your mentor doesn't have to be in the same field as you. This person could be someone from an organization in your industry. It could be a parent or other relative. It could even be a friend who is ahead of the curve on you in business. Whoever it is, it needs to be someone you can talk to on a regular basis, exchange ideas with, and learn from. It has to be someone you know will provide valuable, thoughtful information and advice. Hopefully, this person will be your sounding board for many years to come, but mentors can change as you and your business mature, and that's okay.

Your first conversation should be about your business plan or how you can convert your idea into a business plan. Your next conversation should be about recommendations for the rest of your dream team.

Tax coach and accountant. Think of an accountant like the doctor you see for your yearly checkup. This doctor will analyze your weight, your cholesterol level, your blood pressure, your heart rate, your sugar level, etc. Then he or she will tell you your test results and give you some advice on things you should cut back on or do more of until you see each other again in a year. He or she will monitor you yearly and simply *document* your results.

Now think of a tax coach like a personal trainer. The personal trainer breaks down your yearly health goals into weekly and monthly action lists and teaches you the exercises you need to do and the foods you need to eat. This person works by your side, making sure you execute the proper steps and helping you achieve your goals, and provides the accountability that the MD does not. This way, at the end of the year, when you go for your checkup with the MD, you are healthy.

So the accountant will record, monitor, and prepare your financial documents quarterly and yearly, and the tax coach will strategize and guide you one-on-one throughout the year. Over the years, as you become more knowledgeable, you will need the tax coach less often; however, you will always need the accountant.

Sometimes, your accountant might also be your tax coach, but if your accountant simply "records" what you have done each year, please find yourself a tax coach in addition to your accountant. It's paramount to understand what to do throughout the year so you are prepared at year-end. And being prepared at year-end means you are not only financially legal but also financially solvent.

Some things to cover with the tax coach and the accountant include:

- Determining the best classification for your business. Examples include S-Corp, LLC, and sole proprietorship. There are advantages and disadvantages to each, and you need to understand them to make the proper choice for you.

- Learning how to set up a daily accounting system, whether it's something like FreshBooks or something of your own. The point is, you must have a daily financial system, and you must use it from day one. Don't wait until your first year in business comes to a close and then find out what you were supposed to have done all year long to be ready for the taxman.
- Determining how and when you personally should expect to take a paycheck from your business. It's not uncommon for small business owners to go weeks and months before taking a paycheck. Often this is because you are re-investing the profits into the business, which can be a good thing as long as it's monitored and thoughtfully tracked with specific goals planned. But make no mistake: Running a business is not a hobby. And if you don't earn a living from it, it's a hobby—a very expensive hobby. I always say, if I want a hobby, I'll hit my yoga class! Be intentional about how you will make money from your business.

Lawyer. After you have met with your accountant, you are ready to meet with an attorney. This too will be a lifetime relationship. Interview and select someone you are comfortable with, someone who respects the endeavor you are embarking on, and someone with a good reputation specializing in small business law. Some of the things your attorney will do include:

- Filing your company with the state in the designation you decided with your accountant.
- Filing documents to trademark your business name if desired.
- Applying for any licenses you may need for your field.
- Helping you write the wording for the contracts you will have with your clients, if applicable.
- Reviewing lease agreements for your office or studio space if you are a brick and mortar business.

- Advising you and helping you determine agreements if one partner wants to dissolve or if one partner were to die. I know it's not easy to think of this when you're starting out, but it's so much better to do it now when these things seem like they could never happen. Emotions are not as intrusive now as they can be in crisis.

Marketing expert. Unless you already have a very clear vision of your "brand," you should spend some time working with a marketing strategist who can help you develop and formulate your brand. Your brand is the secret sauce that sets your company apart from all the others that do the same thing. It's your superpower. You have one, and it doesn't need to be exotic.

For example, if you own a fitness center, you could be the only fitness center in the area that caters to the needs of mothers with young children. You go out of your way, from the hours classes are offered to the reception area with enough space to put the moms' coats, the kids' coats, and the diaper bags, to the amenities and supervision on site to keep kids happy while mom works out. Can you immediately picture how different an exercise facility catering to moms would look, feel, and be as compared to a facility geared toward high school and college athletes? When you imagine it, doesn't your mind start to race at all the differences you would expect to find in each space? It may not be a glamorous superpower, but do you think you could lock up all the moms in the area if you did everything you could to maximize the experience for this demographic? You bet you could!

So with your marketing expert, you should cover these items:

- Identifying your brand.
- Developing a story around that brand.
- Developing a strategy to get the message of your brand to your target market.

- Developing your company name, logo, colors, and style to reflect your brand and attract your ideal client.
- Developing your website.
- Developing your printed materials including business cards, letterhead, and thank-you cards.
- Developing your Facebook and Instagram strategies.
- Finding ways to differentiate yourself from the competition in your field.

Bank manager. You must open a business bank account. Unfortunately, I have met many business owners who haven't opened up a business account because they thought they didn't have to worry about it because they didn't have any revenue yet. They foolishly run everything through their personal finances. Please don't do that. Open up a business account.

I urge you, even in this age of ATM banking, online banking, and banking from your telephone, to walk into your neighborhood bank, introduce yourself to the branch manager, and tell that branch manager that you are opening up a business. Ask this person to help you through the process, order the checks, set up your pin numbers, etc. You may be able to do this without the manager, but you want to cultivate a relationship with this person.

Since 1982, my husband has had our business account at the same bank. He goes in every week, in person, to deposit the checks we have received from our clients and other transactions. Over the years, there have been many bank managers and many tellers, but they all have known my husband, at the very least by face, and most often, if they are there long enough, they know him by name as well.

There is tremendous value in your banker knowing who you are. If you go in regularly and develop a relationship, you definitely receive better service.

The first time we faced a recession in our business, my husband took a position at another company for eighteen months so we would survive it. During this period, I handled the bills, the banking, etc.

One day, I got a phone call from the bank manager. "Something doesn't seem right," he said. "Your account hasn't had a deposit in four weeks, and you don't have the funds to cover the checks you have written. Is there something wrong at Window Works?"

I was terrified. How could this happen? What in the world did I do? I explained I had been making deposits all month, and I had all the slips.

The manager said he wasn't sure what was going on, but he was authorizing everything to be paid, and together we would get to the bottom of it. (As far as I was concerned, as long as we did it before I had to tell my husband, I would be happy.)

Later I went to the bank with my deposit slips, and we found that I had picked up a stack of deposit slips from an old, defunct bank account of ours. I had been depositing our checks into that account for weeks and didn't know it. But because my husband had a long-standing relationship with the bank and the manager, we didn't get a notice full of overdraft fees and bounced checks. Instead, the manager called us and paid our checks, even before he knew what happened. He exercised his judgment based on his relationship with my husband. Your mobile phone isn't going to do that for you, so please skip the drive-through and online banking at least 75 percent of the time and get to know the people in your bank.

Another suggestion is to ask the bank manager if you can set up a line of credit. Ask for whatever amount you qualify. If you qualify for a $1,000 line of credit, open a $1,000 line. If you qualify for $10,000 or $20,000, open it up. Understand when you qualify and open the line of credit, as long as you don't draw on it, there is no interest or payment due. To be clear, I'm *not* suggesting that you set up a line of credit and use it to get your business off the ground. You should already have saved your start-up money and your first several months of expenses.

What I'm suggesting is that you set it up and don't spend it. This line of credit is insurance for when something unexpected happens, something you aren't prepared for because in business, something will happen eventually.

Now let's assume that things are going well, and it's been eight or ten months, and you haven't needed the line of credit (which, hopefully, you haven't because you are intentional in your forecasting and your spending). Then spend some of it. Buy a copier, something you need, something well under the credit limit amount, and then pay it off *in full* the next month. This is simply so that the bank sees that you're out there, you're active, and you're responsible. Sometimes when you leave your line of credit dormant for too long, especially when it's new, they reduce it, and then when you do need it, and you may need more, they don't allow you to borrow more because they don't know if you're reliable. This is an important tool for a business owner, and the time to ask for money is when you don't need it, not when you do need it. It always reminds me of the saying: "The time to fix your roof is when the sun is shining." I love that idea.

Negotiable Experts

In addition to the nonnegotiable experts, there are negotiable experts that would benefit your team too.

Webmaster. I recognize that many of you are very tech savvy, and there are many services, such as Wix, WordPress, and Squarespace, that make it relatively easy to build a quality website on your own. However, if you need a custom site with upgraded features, or if you're like me and you don't have the expertise, time, or patience to build a site, then you will need to hire somebody to build it. I know you know you can't do business in this day and age without a website. The first thing people will do when they hear about you and your service is to look for you online. They want to see if what they have heard about you lines up with what they see online. So a webmaster is negotiable as long as you get it done. Do it yourself, or hire somebody to do it for you.

Public Relations (PR) firm. A PR firm is also something to consider. You probably don't need one in the beginning, but it's something to think about down the line depending on your product or service.

Business coach. A business coach is different from a mentor. Your mentor is more likely someone you brainstorm with, someone you share your big ideas with and make broad-stroke plans with, and someone who will pick you up, dust you off, and kick you back out into the world when you need it. The business coach, on the other hand, is actionable. Recall the difference between the accountant and the tax coach. The business coach helps you sort good ideas from bad ones, identifying which ideas are manageable and profitable and merit your time, energy, and money. The business coach will teach you systems and procedures to organize and streamline your business. And the coach will teach you how to set specific goals along with the skills to accomplish them and then, most importantly, hold you accountable.

To find a good coach, ask successful colleagues if they know of one. The coach doesn't have to be in your industry because smart business is smart business. However, there are coaches who specialize within industries too, and that can be beneficial. Another way of finding a coach is through podcasts. Many business podcasters are also business coaches. The sessions are done through Skype or Zoom, so location is not an issue. The great thing about this is you can listen to their shows for weeks, getting to know them and their style to see if they feel like a fit before you hire them.

If you don't have the budget for a coach, a terrific alternative is to join a mastermind group. There are free masterminds and paid masterminds. Depending on your stage in business, either can be appropriate, and both can be valuable.

You can even start your own free mastermind with other entrepreneurs you have met through networking and industry events. Your group decides whether to meet in person or virtually and how often you will meet—weekly, monthly, whatever suits your group. Together you discuss your challenges and compare ideas on how to operate and grow your business. Since there usually is no leader per se, these masterminds tend to be informal, providing a place to connect, share war stories, and ask for advice.

An experienced businessperson, on the other hand, leads paid masterminds. The leader will establish tight rules for the group regarding protocols such as attendance, duration of the mastermind, the frequency of meetings, and the specific time for the meetings. For masterminds that have a two- or three-month duration, you will usually meet weekly. For yearly masterminds, you might meet monthly. In both cases, there will be action items to be completed between each meeting to ensure that each member benefits in a tangible way from the experience. Additionally, each meeting will start exactly at the hour specified and end exactly on time. There is no running over and nothing casual about these masterminds. While they are enjoyable and nurturing, they are and should be well organized and actionable.

Both masterminds and business coaches are available at a wide range. Masterminds can cost from as little as $400 per month all the way to $40,000, $50,000, and $60,000 per year. You might find a business coach who charges $1,000 per month and one who charges $5,000 per month. Interestingly, in the many conversations I have had with seven- and eight-figure earners, I have found that most have either a business coach or a high-level paid mastermind, and often they have both. It seems pretty logical that if people can put down this kind of money for these services, they are probably already super successful at running their business. So when smart, successful people do something, it's something to notice.

According to one survey, "70 percent of the companies that had used small business coaching believed business coaching is 'very valuable.'"[5] Think about that; not 10 percent, not 5 percent, but 70 percent find it valuable. Also when they were working with a business coach,

- 62.4 percent of the business owners felt they were better at smarter goal-setting
- 60.5 percent of the business owners felt they had a more balanced life
- 57.1 percent of the business owners felt they had lower stress levels[6]

Understand that if you have been in business for one, three, five years, you probably don't need the same business coach or mastermind as a multimillionaire with a seven-figure income. But the lesson is how valuable coaching and masterminds can be for all of us, at every stage of our business. This is particularly important if you are a solopreneur without a partner to bounce ideas around with. So as a new entrepreneur, try to embrace the value of this, and make it a goal to include one-on-one coaching or a mastermind as a line item in your budget just like marketing, insurances, utilities, and overhead.

Tech or computer consultant. The final expert you want to include on your dream team is a tech or computer consultant. Like the other experts I have recommended, this is not a full-time hire; this is a consultant to be paid when needed. And I strongly urge you not to rely on a family member or friend. A savvy family member or friend is someone you can talk with on the weekends or at night and ask his or her advice on how to set up a spreadsheet or download a software

---

5   "Is Small Business Coaching Worthwhile?" (n.d.). Retrieved December 12, 2016, from http://businessknowledgesource.com/smallbusiness/is_small_business_coaching_worthwhile_027827.html

6   "Is Small Business Coaching Worthwhile?" (n.d.). Retrieved December 12, 2016, from http://businessknowledgesource.com/smallbusiness/is_small_business_coaching_worthwhile_027827.html

program. The tech or computer consultant is someone who will show up in an emergency during the workday because it is his or her work to do exactly this. Imagine that one day, there are no new emails or your Word or Excel programs aren't working, and you need to get proposals out. If you don't know how to solve such problems, and you don't have a twenty-five-year-old working for you who knows how to do it, then there must be somebody you can call who will come ASAP.

I've had that happen in my business more times than I can count. I couldn't have relied on my nephew or somebody with his own job because I needed help right then, not after their workday. When your business is in jeopardy tech-wise, you need to be able to call somebody for immediate help and get the problem resolved.

The above experts will become your extended team. You will need them to be your best and to give your best to your clients. It's perfectly fine not to know everything connected to running your business. There is no shame in that. You have your role, the things you do better than anyone else; do those and do them well. For the other things, ask for help, hire in-house, and contract outside vendors. Create the ideal team to be by your side throughout your business life. It will bring you peace of mind, and it will foster your growth and success.

CHAPTER 3

Be a Systems Freak

In this chapter, we will talk about systems. Systems are the backbone of *every* business, whether it's a food cart at the carnival or a multimillion-dollar business. Systems are the processes by which you organize and manage the information flow in and out of your company. When you take the time to think about your goals for every task, you can develop the most efficient ways to handle these tasks, creating time, efficiency, and peace of mind. Without systems, you will repeat efforts, you will feel chaotic, you will feel unsure, and you will feel unclear about your direction. And you will be right about those feelings.

The time to wrangle this beast is from the beginning when you are starting out. There are two very good reasons for this. The first is very simply that you need to spend your time creating new revenue, not chasing an endless circle of unorganized invoices, phone calls, and to-do lists. The second is that when it's time to onboard your first employee, this person can hit the ground running because you have established a clear roadmap of how and what you do, making training infinitely easier. It will be at minimum difficult and likely impossible to scale and grow your business without systems in place. You can't be the only one who does something, and you can't be the only one who knows how to do something.

What does your business look like now? Do you have a system for placing an order, for following up on open projects, and for paying your bills? The fact of the matter is that when you run a business, you are likely to do a lot of the same tasks every day. However, if you are not doing them in the same order and the same way every time, you will forget or skip things. If you come into your office in the morning, and you do the first task, the fifth task, the sixth task, then the second task, and at the end of one hour, you have done all ten tasks that are associated with one particular thing you're doing, that's terrific. But what happens if you get a phone call or you get interrupted in some other way? Do you forget that you haven't completed one part?

We have lots of systems at Window Works. Even our systems have systems. One of the key components is that a process performed by one team member is designed to oversee a process by another team member. Or if you are solo, you would have a system for one process that includes a crosscheck of a previous step. For example, we have an invoice for ordering custom window treatments and awnings. The invoice has eight lines for writing in the products to be ordered, and the bottom right corner of the invoice has a small box also with eight lines. Once I've placed the order with the vendor for each of the eight lines, I have to write down in the smaller box. Line one, I emailed it, line two, I faxed it, and line three, I phone called it. If there are reference numbers associated with these orders, I note them all down in the small box. Then I turn the invoice over to my showroom manager who puts all the information into our computer system. At this point, she has her own processes to employ, and one includes that she verifies that every line on the order has corresponding information in the small box. Every once in a while, she brings me an invoice and says, "I don't see where you ordered line four." Ah, nice catch! Back it goes to me to be completed. If this system were not in place, we could be four weeks into an order and have received everything except an item never ordered, which would delay everything four weeks.

So, you see, systems produce two things for your business—a productive workflow as well as a fail-safe. They are the inherent double checks for finding mistakes and therefore are a huge aid in avoiding problems wherever possible.

It reminds me of when my children were little, and we would read the book *If You Give a Mouse a Cookie*. *If You Give a Mouse a Cookie* reads,

> "If a hungry little mouse shows up on your doorstep, you might want to give him a cookie. And if you give him a cookie, he'll ask for a glass of milk. He'll want to look in a mirror to make sure he doesn't have a milk mustache, and then he'll ask for a pair of scissors to give himself a trim . . ."[7]

The mouse goes on to ask for the next thing and the next. If you have raised children, you know that sometimes when you read a nighttime story, you skip a few pages in the book. The funny thing about this book is that you can't skip any pages because your kids will call you out on it. "No, no, Mommy, you didn't do the napkin page." The little mouse has a system for eating his cookies, and you need a system for every task too.

Don't assume that a phone call won't interrupt you. Don't assume that when you are tired and finish at eight o'clock at night and your children come in and want you to read them a story, you're going to remember the next day what you did or didn't do. Systemize your steps so you can double-check yourself.

How to Create the Systems

To create systems for your business, start by breaking down everything you do in a day. What are the reoccurring tasks associated with running your business? What do you do daily, weekly, quarterly, and yearly?

7   Numeroff, L.J. (2010). *If You Give a Mouse a Cookie*. New York: HarperCollins Publishers.

When I say everything, I mean everything. Start with how you answer the telephone. If there is a way you want your phone answered, document it. In my business, we all must say our name in our greeting. The greeting isn't as important to me as saying your name. (It irritates me when you call a company, and you don't know who you are speaking with.) Then there are companies that require all of their people to answer the phone by saying, "Hello, it's a great day at, name of the company." Think about it, something as simple as the way the phone is answered, if it's not decided, will be done every which way. This is the first contact with your clients, and you want it to be consistent, professional, and phrased how you want. It sets the tone for the rest of your clients' experience with you.

Another simple task is how your employees take messages for you. I can't stand it when I get a message that doesn't have a telephone number with it. I don't want to have to look for the number. It's a small thing, but it saves time and improves efficiency. Also, messages must be in our message book. Messages written on scrap paper get lost, and that's not good.

How do you handle your emails? Have you established a time frame for how quickly they must be answered? Is it within one day, two days? If you don't have a guideline for this, you will find out that customers could be waiting three days, four days, five days, or a week for an answer to their emails. Establish standards.

If you have outside salespeople who call on people, what is their protocol? What do they wear? How do they introduce themselves at the clients' homes or at their place of business? How do they follow up with the clients and within what time frame? Do you want them to send a thank-you card for having a meeting or for a closed sale?

You also need systems for your finances. What do you do when you get new invoices? What do you do with paid invoices? How do you invoice clients? Keeping track of the money is vital. I have met far too many small business owners who don't take the time to carefully review invoices coming into or leaving their business. It would be impossible for me to guess at how many times in thirty plus years a vendor has billed us incorrectly. And when I think of the number of times colleagues have told me that they never crosscheck their vendor's invoices, that they simply pay the amount on the bill every month, it makes me cringe. People make mistakes, and when you overpay, you are plain and simply throwing your hard-earned money out the door.

In the area of monitoring our money, we have several systems, overlapping with checks and balances between team members just like our other systems. Every staff member who handles financial transactions with our clients has a specific protocol to follow.

One such system is for our "to be paid" invoices. We have three checkpoints for every product-related invoice we pay, and they are:

1. Our showroom coordinator is responsible for looking up prices from a vendor's catalog and order confirmation to ensure that both the products and the dollar amount listed for each line item is accurate. She does this every week on Thursday—not Monday, not the Thursdays she feels like it, every Thursday.

2. After our showroom coordinator has indicated that all entries are correct, the invoice goes to my husband who reviews it again for accuracy before he pays it.

3. The invoice goes to whichever salesperson the products ordered are connected to. This salesperson reviews it once more to be sure it lists only items ordered for this customer.

Operating invoices, such as utilities, phone, office supplies, insurances, and similar, go through the two checkpoints of our showroom coordinator and my husband. For these types of bills, they both check and compare to the previous month or year to be certain there are no unusual hikes in price or add-ons. We have caught phone bills with added amounts for features we were not using. The number of errors in invoicing you find when you pay attention as closely as we do is truly mind-boggling.

Unfortunately, the reverse can be true as well; we can make errors in collecting the monies due to us. We were guilty of this too at Window Works until my husband developed the *Red Pen System*.

The Red Pen System is our daily financial accounting system where we track deposits on every new order and balance dues on every completed installation. Here is how it works. First, no one except my husband and me is allowed to use a red pen in our office. You can't use a red pen to make a note on a scratch pad, an invoice to a customer, an invoice from a vendor—nothing, nada, zippo, it's not happening, not allowed. Only Vin and I can use a red pen. And we can only use it for one thing: to indicate on every customer invoice that we have received the customer's deposit and the customer's balance due. No notes about installation detail, no notes to the showroom coordinator, nothing. The system has various steps to it, but the ultimate objective is to give Vin a way, at a glance, to see if we have in fact collected every deposit and every balance due from every customer.

I'll just take a moment to caution you here: If you don't have a system for monitoring that you have been paid by your clients, you have likely missed one if not several payments due to you every year you have been in business. How do I know this? Because we developed the Red Pen System specifically because every year at our annual end-of-year customer invoice analysis (another system we have related to our finances), we had multiple orders where monies had not been collected. Even after Vin came up with this system, we would still discover at least one or two each year. The number had come down from six, seven, or eight, but still, who wants to leave any money on the table? This is not a hobby, remember? But as the years have gone by and the system has been perfected and has become ingrained, it has now been many years since Vin has discovered unpaid invoices. I still remember the last time it happened; it was about eight years ago. During his January review, he found an order we had installed and completed the previous April but never collected the $1,200 balance on. When we called these clients, they did a dance about not remembering and needing to check their records, but a week or so after they had looked into their records and not been able to produce a canceled check or a payment on a credit card statement, we collected our money—because of Vin's Red Pen System.

How to Document Them

The best time to document each process in your business is when you are in the middle of it. First, you do this, then you do that, and there is your system. If you are a terrific typist, you can create an employee-training manual in a Word document. There is also software, such as Camtasia and ScreenFlow, you can download on your computer. It will take screenshots of your monitor and record your voice, so you can talk through an entire process to your computer. So, for example, if you are placing orders with your vendors online, you can just open up the screen with a vendor and describe every step you take, and then that can be saved as a video for training your employees. If you do this for every system you have, you will eventually have either a training manual or a video log of all your systems.

The Benefits of Establishing Systems

Only when you have established systems can you easily duplicate yourself. And if your goal is to grow your business, then understand right out of the gate that your goal is to duplicate yourself. It's fairly well agreed that if you are a solopreneur, even if you work from your third-floor bedroom, your revenues will go up with the first assistant you hire. And yet most solopreneurs resist hiring that first assistant, putting it off until well after they knew they needed one. Why is this? Well, most are worried that they won't be able to pay them, they are unsure of what the assistant will do, and ultimately, they are anxious to take on the responsibility for fear of wasting time and money. But if you have established your systems, you can onboard the new employee quickly and seamlessly. You can trade feeling overwhelmed by too many tasks and feeling clueless about what the new employee will do with getting on to increasing your productivity and your revenues. Documented systems are the answer to your productivity both in the doing and in the teaching. That's the big message. When you hire employees, you can go through the manual or the video with them, and then they can go back to it as many times as they need to learn exactly how the systems work. You don't need to spoon feed and handhold all new hires while they get up to speed on how to operate in your business.

When you have clear, finite systems in place, it not only makes it easy for you to train your employees, but it also makes it easy for any employees to train new employees. If everyone answers the phone the same way and corresponds with the vendor the same way and when everyone knows what the standards are, then it's easy for everybody, not just you, to help each other.

Also, with proper systems in place, your business can run even when you aren't in the office, whether it's a scheduled absence or an emergency absence. Everybody knows what happens at Window Works whether we're in the building or not. The business runs the same way for the duration of our vacations or our emergencies. Big decisions can always be put on hold, but the daily workflow keeps going as usual. Our employees know what we expect and how to do it, and therefore they have confidence in the decisions they make in our absence. Clear systems are a tremendous gift to your employees and clients because they create a less stressful environment when you are away.

Everyone in your company has to follow the systems every day in every way, for every task. Your business will run much smoother and more efficiently if everyone is on board with your systems. Over time, your systems become part of your brand and your culture. This is comforting and valuable to both your clients and your employees. You don't want someone screaming, "You didn't read the napkin part, Mommy. You didn't read the glass of milk part, Mommy."

Another critical benefit earned by establishing systems for your business is that at some point in your career, you will want to retire, and you might like to sell your business rather than simply close it. If you are a new entrepreneur, you might think you don't need to worry about this yet. However, the beginning of your business is exactly the time when you should be thinking about this. It's so much easier to prepare and plan for the future than to find yourself unprepared. I promise you, you don't want to be in business for twenty-five or thirty years and then try to figure out if your business is sellable and, more importantly, positioned for sale. You might not even be at retirement age when you decide to sell your business. Perhaps your business is just three or four years old, and you are looking at a new opportunity.

If your business is successful, well run, and systemized, it could be a very attractive opportunity for someone else. When evaluating a business for sale, smart buyers will look at several criteria, and one of these will undoubtedly include, "Can it run without the outgoing owner?" Your manual or video will show the potential buyers that you have instilled systems that will allow them to continue doing what you have done. In other words, it shows that when you walk out the door, a business with a direction and a roadmap remains. This is extremely valuable.

I always say that a business without systems is a "you," not a business. A business is an entity that includes, among other things, a customer base, a set of systems, and assets that can be purchased and continue to exist and thrive. A "you" is something that possibly includes a client base and assets, but no one but you knows who they are, what they are, or how to access and manage them in order to create revenue and profit. The only way an outsider can determine the value of your business is by looking at your documented customer base, preferably an email list, documented systems and processes, and accurate financial records detailing the fiscal health of the business. Your benchmark is that someone can come in and learn to operate your business without you there. If your admin can teach someone the core of your business, you are on the right track. But if you are the only one who knows how to do everything, you are on a runaway train in the wrong direction.

So start off from day one preparing your business for the next owner. It's like that car commercial where the one person says to the other person, "Please take good care of our car; I'm the second owner."

CHAPTER 4

How to Find Your Clients

To find your ideal clients, answer these questions: Who are you and who do you serve?

If you ask *successful* business owners to describe their ideal clients, I guarantee they will have a succinct answer for you. Why? Because knowing who your ideal clients are is critical to building your client base and your success. To do something even as simple as order business cards, you should have spent considerable time answering this question.

Begin with You

To answer this question, begin with *who are you*? Go back to your company mission, to your *why*. Why are you doing what you are doing? What part of your work brings you the most joy, the most satisfaction? When are you happy, challenged, and jazzed up? By knowing yourself, you can find the people you are driven to help, who you align with, the people who your services and products serve, the people who most want your products and services. These are your ideal clients. With this information, you can develop marketing strategies, customer service strategies, a company name, a logo, and a company culture—all to attract your ideal clients right to you.

Using the earlier example of the fitness center, let's consider an entrepreneur who wants to open a health club.

Based on his or her specific personality and particular *why*, here are just a few health-club demographics:

- Moms, twenty-five to forty years old
- Teens involved in high school sports teams
- Bodybuilders training for competitions
- Sidelined athletes of all ages returning to sports
- People recovering from injuries and diseases
- Women only, noncompetitive environment catering to the new workout enthusiast
- Sport specific: yoga, Pilates, CrossFit, boot camp, kickboxing, Zumba, spin cycling
- Family-friendly gyms with amenities such as family locker rooms etc.

This is just off the top of my head; I'm sure I could go on. But, hopefully, you see how important it is to identify what your expertise is, what you want to do, and how you will serve your demographic. It is the only way to determine how to attract them to you.

Think about it, if you had a fitness center catering to new moms, and your friend had a gym catering to serious hard-core athletes, could anything be the same in each of your businesses?

- Would your marketing plan be the same?
- Would the types of trainers be the same?
- Would the equipment in the facilities be the same?
- Would the locker room amenities be the same?
- Would they both have locker rooms?
- Could they both be called a gym? Could they both be called a fitness center? Don't these two words convey something very different?

Can you see how getting clarity on you, your business, and who you serve will shape every decision from the name of your business to your business cards, your print advertising, your social media presence, and the way you dress? Every last detail should be considered to maximize every opportunity to be successful.

Most importantly, can you understand why it's okay and actually best if you don't try to be all things to all people? Can you effectively serve both bodybuilders and new moms? No, you can't! Neither group wants to work out together. So pick your tribe and leave the rest behind. Don't worry about leaving people out; speak loudly, clearly, and directly to your people, and they will come. The smaller and more clearly defined your niche is, the easier it will be to develop a loyal, engaged customer base.

When you are clear on your vision, who you serve, how you help your ideal clients, and the clients who bring you the most joy, you can build your following—your client base—and grow your business because you are laser focused.

How Do You Define You?

I suggest you start by making a list of every sub-niche in your business category, like we did in the example of the health club above. Go deep; go further than you think you need to. As you saw, in the fitness category, I listed fourteen subcategories, and I know I could find more. Don't overlook even the smallest niche in your area of expertise. Not sure it's worth the trouble? Consider SoulCycle.

Who would have thought, with a health club in nearly every town and with cycling classes included in the memberships, you could offer only cycling and at a more expensive per-class rate than almost any yoga class around. I mean, you're offering stationary bike classes—not exactly reinventing the wheel, or aren't you? Take a look at what *The New York Times* wrote about SoulCycle:

But while the math is simple, SoulCycle's profit margins are surprising. If it has found a way to mint money, competitors should be able to swarm into the fancy indoor cycling world and beat it on price. This is not a business with high barriers to entry: Full-line gyms like New York Sports Clubs offer cycling classes to their members for no additional charge. In short, Economics 101 says SoulCycle's high profit margin should be eaten away by competition.[8]

And it goes on to say:

SoulCycle does seem to offer something unique: a sense that what it sells is more than a workout. Devotees of the chain cite benefits from their engagement with SoulCycle that go well beyond the physical.

"It's sold convincingly and addictively as personal growth and therapeutic progress through fitness," said Ben Dreyfuss, the engagement editor at Mother Jones magazine, who lives in Manhattan and estimates he has taken an average of one SoulCycle class a day for the last 45 days. "It's got the calming bits of yoga mixed with the group pack mentality of team sports and the weird psychological whatever you want to call it of following a squad leader into battle."[9]

SoulCycle has defined a specific niche, and they have created a business model that attracts exactly the client they desire.

Suppose we were to make a brainstorming worksheet for a generic fitness club. It might look like this:

8   Barro, J. (2015, August 7). SoulCycle: Your Say 'Cult.' I Say 'Loyal Customer Base.' *The New York Times*. Retrieved October 20, 2017, from https://www.nytimes.com/2015/08/09/upshot/soulcycle-you-say-cult-i-say-loyal-customer-base.html

9   Barro, J. (2015, August 7). SoulCycle: Your Say 'Cult.' I Say 'Loyal Customer Base.' *The New York Times*. Retrieved October 20, 2017, from https://www.nytimes.com/2015/08/09/upshot/soulcycle-you-say-cult-i-say-loyal-customer-base.html

Fitness club

• coed • male only • female only • competitive • supportive • budget friendly • high end • sport specific • general fitness • noncompetitive • group classes • private training • other services offered, e.g. massage, sauna, café • family friendly • babysitting • mommy and me • student athletes • senior friendly • body only • connect body and mind • early hours • late-night hours • 24 hours • boutique feeling • intimate • luxury • designed interiors • no frills • busy beehive feeling • hands off • anonymity • all ages comfortable •personalized • encouraging • involved • equipment, machines • orchestrate interaction between members • exclusive • membership only • pay-as-you-go option •results orientated • cultivate community • take time to know patrons • offer classes and activities to appeal to everyone • concentrate on one specialty • state of the art in every way • hip, modern feeling • industrial feeling • all business no play vibe •

Now, if you were focusing on designing a fitness center like SoulCycle, what might you pull from this list?

Fitness club

• **coed** • male only • female only • competitive • **supportive** • budget friendly • **high end** • **sport specific** • general fitness • **noncompetitive** • **group classes** • private training • other services offered, e.g. massage, sauna, café • family friendly • babysitting • mommy and me • student athletes • senior friendly • body only • **connect body and mind** • **early hours** • late-night hours • 24 hours • **boutique feeling** • intimate • **luxury** • **designed interiors** • no frills • busy beehive feeling • hands off • anonymity • all ages comfortable •personalized • **encouraging** • **involved** • **equipment, machines** • orchestrate interaction between members • exclusive • membership only • **pay-as-you-go option** •results orientated • **cultivate community** • **take time to know patrons** • offer classes and activities to appeal to everyone • concentrate on one specialty

• state of the art in every way • hip, modern feeling • industrial feeling • all business no play vibe •

Starting with the bolded list, you would go further into each of these items and decide what each description means *to you* and how will you achieve it. Let's take just two categories from above. First, the obvious, sport specific. In this example, that would be cycling. Second, cultivate community. You could encourage interaction and multiple visits to your website by providing valuable health information or fitness related information in a company blog. Then you could show fun, inspiring photos of members enjoying classes. You could cultivate community further by organizing outside riding events and get-togethers with members. Also, you could offer "get you started" classes for newbies to lessen their anxiety. Then you could sell clothing and gear with logos to encourage the members' ownership of your brand. Lastly, you could put your mission statement on your home page to encourage the members' connection with the brand further and share detailed profiles with pictures of your instructors.

Do you see how you start to build a profile of your company with exercises like these? It can be done for any industry. In my industry, there are no-frills companies selling window treatments and no-frills companies selling awnings, but these are not our competition. These companies have no auxiliary services. You take your measurements and then, either in the store or online, you have to decipher the product that is best for you. These companies don't provide professional advice on the advantages and disadvantages of the various styles based on your personal needs. And when your product is shipped to you, you have to install it. Our business, by contrast, is full-service for both our window treatments and awnings. We go to our clients' homes, we provide ideas and critical guidance about the myriad of options, we take the measurements, we place and receive the orders, and finally, our trained full-time installers install the treatments and awnings. We have no desire or need to compete with companies that don't provide auxiliary services because we have identified who we want to sell to. We serve and work with only those who require, value, and appreciate a full-service experience. I don't have any judgment on the low, middle, or high end of any industry. The no-frills blind and awning companies I described have a terrific, viable business model that works.

It's the same with Target and Bloomingdale's, right? Both stores sell shoes, clothing, and home goods, but there is no similarity in the styles and brands they offer and absolutely no similarity in their price points. However, both are very successful. It's because they know their brand and who their ideal clients are. They cater to their people and leave the others behind. We all know there is room—in fact, a true need—for both types in the marketplace. My point is, pick your place.

Define Your Ideal Clients

When you have identified your "you," what your superpower is and how you will carry it out, you have defined your brand, which informs everything you do. With this information, you can now work toward finding the people who want your services and products, the people your brand speaks to.

To define your ideal clients, answer these questions:

- Who likes, wants, or needs the service or product you offer?
- What kind of work do they do?
- What do they earn?
- What car do they drive?
- What stores do they shop in?
- What kind of home do they live in?
- What education do they have?
- Do they have kids?
- Do they own their home or rent?
- What organizations are they involved in?
- What do they do in their leisure time?

- Where do they vacation?
- What kind of restaurants do they go to?
- What kind of books and magazines do they read?
- Do they exercise?
- How old are they?
- What schools do their kids go to?

Write out the list. Get extremely specific. Leave off no detail. If it's difficult for you to make the list, think about one or two of your favorite clients. Picture them and their everyday lives in great detail, and then go back to the list and answer each question.

Find Them

Now that you know who you are and who your ideal clients are, you have to find them. Again, visualize your clients' lifestyle very closely.

Where do your ideal clients spend time?

- Are they online? If yes, where? Are they on Facebook, Instagram, Twitter, LinkedIn, or Pinterest? These are all very different platforms, each with their own culture. Your ideal clients may be on two or three, but it's unlikely they are on all of them.
- Do they rely on local newspapers for their information?
- Do they look for and respond to direct mail coupon books?
- Are they in local organizations?
- Are they in mom groups or the parent-teacher association (PTA)?
- Do they go to networking events or are they in a business network international (BNI) chapter, a chamber of commerce, or a trade association?
- Do they learn about your type of products and services strictly through referrals from friends and family?

Market to Them

Okay, we're finally getting somewhere. You know who you are, you know who your ideal clients are, and you know where they are. Now let's go get them. Align everything you do with your ideal clients' values and ideals—everything from your logo to your business card, your product packaging, your invoicing, your storefront or studio, your reception area, your car, the hours you are open or available, all the way down to your phone greeting and the way you and your staff are dressed.

Going back to the comparison between Target and Bloomingdale's, let's examine the shoe department in each store. At Target, there are racks of shoes organized by size but not by style, it's self-service, and there is possibly a little stool to sit on—and let's not forget about those plastic loops holding the pairs of shoes together! You can't even walk in the shoes to test the fit without doing a Tim Conway shuffle. (If you are too young to know what that is, go to YouTube and search *The Carol Burnett Show*, "The Oldest Fireman with Tim Conway"—it's hilarious!) At Bloomingdale's, the shoe department emotes luxury. It feels like a beautifully designed living room. It has comfortable sofas, chairs, tables to put your bags on, lamps for ambient lighting, and full-length mirrors everywhere. The salespeople will fetch you every style and size you need. Every detail has been considered to get you to slow down, to browse, and to try on as many shoes as you want, hopefully encouraging you to leave with all of them. For certain, both companies sell shoes, but the experience they provide is completely different, and therefore the marketing message must be carefully constructed to attract the right consumer.

How about the advertisements of each company? Let's compare the print marketing for each. Target's print materials are bold, bright, and filled with pictures of kids, parents, pets, and deals! Their models are approachable; they could be your family and neighbors. Well, okay, they may be a little prettier than your average family, but you could be friends with them. Bloomingdale's print materials are high end, filled with young, glamorous models, women who are six feet tall standing with men who are even taller, and you're not sure which of the two is more beautiful, am I right? These models look like they are stepping off yachts just for a few brief moments to show us their gorgeous clothing and jewelry and to let us know what their favorite cologne is, dahling.

Both work though, right? Because you know what the funny thing is, at different times you probably are the ideal client for each store. Sometimes it depends on what you are buying and what you want from the experience. Each store has done such a great job developing their unique branding message that you know when you want one over the other. Meaning, often times a woman will shop at Bloomie's for clothing and shoes for herself or for special occasions but will shop elsewhere for basics or for her kids. However, this consumer still wants a certain experience and atmosphere. Target is a budget-conscious category, yet they present a clean, stylized, hip atmosphere. Notice how they position for an overlap with the Bloomie's client.

Let's do another comparison—Target and Walmart. Both sell children's clothing at a budget price point. But picture it; Target has bright, pleasing lighting, wide aisles, and stylized mini departments for children, babies, men, and women. Whereas Walmart has dim, warehouse-level lighting and rows of aisles arranged more like a Home Depot or a big box club store. Even though our Bloomingdale's shopper sometimes wants a budget price point, she still wants a feeling that aligns with her ideals, and Target answers that. We can further guess that if and when this same woman does go to Walmart, it's likely for cleaning supplies or groceries and less likely for clothing for her or her kids. It's all good. As I said earlier, every market demographic is valuable and worthy; if you find yours and you stay in your lane, you'll be just fine.

CHAPTER 5

The Key to Profitable Selling: Own Your Worth

There may be a moment when you look around and think: "I'm working very hard and yet somehow I can't seem to make ends meet; why am I struggling so much?" Or maybe "I can't get to the next level." This could be a result of misdirected marketing, out-of-line operating expenses, poor-quality products, or any number of other tangible things. But before we look at them, let's take a moment to be sure you are not the reason you aren't succeeding.

Are you struggling with a mindset problem?

If you are good at what you do, you like doing it, and you're not earning enough money, then maybe you are not charging enough for your services.

Here are some questions to consider:

- Are you afraid that if you raise your prices, you won't land the clients or close the deals?
- Are you afraid that if you present a price to clients, they will ask you why it's so expensive?
- Are you afraid you will get a reputation for being overpriced?

- Is it possible you actually know you are not charging enough and yet you are still afraid to charge your worth?

Let's talk about ways you can overcome this problem.

Step 1: Assess Yourself and Your Value Proposition

Start by making a list of all the services you and your company provide your clients. On one side, list the service, and on the other side, list why and how it benefits your clients. That second part is key because a particular action might not seem like a big deal to you, but when you picture the benefit to your clients, you can grasp its value, even with little services. Everything and anything you do for your clients—list it.

To get your brain clicking, here's a quick list of some services you might already be providing your clients. Make your own list and be sure to make that second list too, the benefits to your client.

- You provide email confirmations of appointments
- You have evening and weekend hours
- You provide initial exploratory phone calls or appointments
- You provide in-home or office consultations, delivery, follow up
- You have X years' experience in the industry
- You attend conferences to stay on top of trends and technology
- You take continuing education units
- You return all phone calls within twenty-four hours
- You have a stated satisfaction guaranteed policy
- You have a stated service or repair policy
- You provide status checks during your clients' projects with you
- You provide expert advice, suggestions, project plans
- You have a "thank you for your referral" protocol

- You have a "thank you for your business" protocol

Take the first example—you provide email confirmations of appointments. That's easy to do; in fact, you can automate it so you aren't even "doing" it. But consider the busy clients who get a reminder the day before an appointment. They know you're coming so they won't have to debate whether they should confirm to avoid running home only to have no one show up. It's a little thing that has a big impact on a busy person's day. I love it.

We often overlook the little ways we enrich our clients' experience because we are accustomed to doing it, and we fall into the trap of underestimating its importance to our clients. By making this list, you should already be feeling a bit more confident about handling price objections and your fear of facing these objections. You should be having a moment of: "Wow, it's pretty awesome to do business with me. I really go out of my way for my clients." I'll bet you'll even realize there are services and amenities that you provide that your competitors do not. When you truly know your value and worth, and you step into it, you will forever forgo the need to discount your products or services. Period.

A couple of years ago, a prospective client called us at Window Works and asked my showroom coordinator for some general information about our company. After she was satisfied with the information she received, she asked for an appointment to see me.

We met at her home, and we were chatting about her master bedroom and master bathroom. She had had someone else do work in the master bath, and she wasn't fully satisfied with the outcome. She was grilling me a bit about what I thought of it and what would I have done. Next, she asked me for advice for her master bedroom. After asking my usual litany of questions about needs regarding light control, privacy, energy efficiency, etc., I made suggestions on what treatments I thought would be best.

We were dancing, and I knew it. It was very friendly, but she was comparing me to the other expert, evaluating if I knew my stuff, and truthfully, that's always okay with me. In fact, I respect consumers who do their homework. They value their money and their home, which in the end, I know will be good for me too because I value their money and their home as well.

At one point, I asked her how she had learned about Window Works, and she explained it was through the newcomer's Facebook group in their town. Oh, okay, I thought to myself, this is really great because I know we have a stellar reputation in this group. So I pressed on, "What a great resource that group is. It's so helpful when you move into town to have such honest feedback about retailers and tradesmen, right?"

"Yes," she agreed, "it has been a lifesaver. When I asked about recommendations for window treatments, I was a bit surprised at how many people recommended you. In less than twenty minutes, about sixteen of the twenty or so responses said good things about you and your company."

"Oh, how nice—for me anyway," I said, laughing.

She laughed too and then said, "Well, not everything was so good."

"No, what do you mean?"

"Well," she went on, "some said yes, you did good work, but you were also expensive. And others just said, 'They are expensive.'" She stopped talking and looked me right in the eyes.

I calmly returned her look and said, "The others who recommended us without qualification, what things did they say about Window Works if I might ask?"

She explained, "Oh, yes, well, practically every person, to a one, said that your company provides tremendous service. You, in particular, have excellent ideas for designing window treatments, your installers are knowledgeable and respectful, you are family owned and have been in business for decades, and the owners really care about their customers and their business."

I looked at her quite directly and said: "And do you want to give up all of that for a lower price?"

She looked back at me for a moment and said: "No, no I don't."

We went on to work together for many months. First, we re-did the master bathroom; then we did her master bedroom, family room, dining room, kitchen, laundry, and daughter's room. Since then, she has referred us to several of her friends. I would say we have both been very pleased we met each other!

Step 2: Don't Charge Based on *Your* Need

Another reason you might be struggling to be profitable is that you are pricing based on your needs rather than your quality, value, and expertise. *You need* to pay the rent; *you need* to make payroll; *you need* to close a sale. You could be so overwhelmed in your business that you don't see the real needs. The real needs are the needs of your potential clients. *They need* your product; *they need* your services; *they need* a problem solved. These are the needs to focus on, not yours. Selling out of your needs will almost always result in underselling and undervaluing your products and services.

Take your emotions out of it. Look at the big picture, and understand that your potential clients have no idea of your need to make a rent payment. They evaluate whether to buy based on your price combined with the value you offer. To calculate your value, they consider your reputation, your references, your expertise, your knowledge, and the quality of the goods, not your overdue rent. Don't lose an opportunity for a profitable sale because of your own fears. The price for your time, your products, and your services is determined based on a formula that includes the net cost of goods, the value and expertise you bring, your operating expenses, and the market price for the product—not how much money you owe in a particular week.

I know it's not easy. And believe me, I know there will be times when you genuinely have your back against a wall. But your potential clients don't know this. Ask for the money you know you deserve and explain why and how you are worth it. Trust in what you do. Some will go with another company, but many more will buy from you. Express how and why you are the one to solve their problems, the one to make things easier, better, prettier, happier, faster, more productive for them. And then do it. When you do this well, you will close sales.

It is about them; it's not about you.

I promise the more you understand and believe you have priced yourself fairly and you trust it, the more sales you will make. Selling at a higher net profit means you will be happier because you have money to run your business, and your clients will be happier because you can afford to provide stellar service. Now you can truly say to your clients you will be there when they need follow-up service because, as a profitable business, you will be open for many years to come.

Soon you will feel the difference in your confidence, and when you combine that with the difference in your checkbook, you won't go back to pricing out of need or scarcity. Sometimes you might have to act as if you have a full checkbook and a full pipeline, and that's okay.

Step 3: Charge Your Worth

The other side of this is to practice and prepare yourself to walk away when someone is unwilling to pay what you're worth. Remember, not everyone is your customer. Unless you are a big-box store or a dollar-type store whose business model is built on selling huge volumes at reduced prices, this is not the way to position yourself.

Most service industries and most professionals are better served by having fewer clients who pay more money than by having more clients who pay less money. Think about it, when you have fewer, more profitable clients, you can provide much better service to these clients. You can go out of your way for them; you can be responsive to their needs and even anticipate their needs. And when you do that, these clients remember you and become advocates for your company. They tell other people about your great service, your great product, and your attention to detail.

To be clear, I'm not suggesting you overcharge anybody; I only want to encourage you to stop undercharging. By undercharging, you are doing a disservice to both you and your clients. When you undercharge and stack your pipeline with too many projects because so many want to take advantage of your ridiculously low price, everyone suffers. It's difficult to provide a quality experience for your clients when your company is pressed beyond its capacity. This is stressful to you as an owner with pride in your business, and it also puts your clients at risk of being lost in the shuffle because you are overwhelmed with more projects than you can handle. You underpriced for fear of not being able to stay in business, and now you risk going out of business because you can't handle and maintain your clients.

To thrive, not just survive, you must provide excellent value and service to everyone. When you provide your best, your clients feel valued and appreciated, and you not only earn repeat business but also earn the highest form of flattery, a referral.

There is no prize for being the least expensive person on the block, but there are tons of prizes for being a leader in your industry and for being known as the company that brings their A-game to every project. Your clients' prize is the exceptional work you do. Your prize is getting to charge your worth. And remember, your clients, not you, determine value. Their idea of expensive is not the same as yours. Do everything you can to create value so they want to do business with you rather than someone else.

Don't underestimate the intangible benefit to both you and your clients. All your clients want to feel special and attended to, and you want to make them feel that way. When you are profitable, you can be their hero.

I hope you can see how this practice results in both higher net profits for you and happier, more satisfied clients. Remember my example from above—most people don't want to exchange customer service, quality products, and personal attention for lower prices.

I'd also like to touch back on the formula I mentioned before. Price is determined by the combination of the net cost of goods, the value and expertise required to perform or deliver the product or service, your operating expenses, and the market value of the product. This means that charging your worth applies to all price levels, not just exclusive or high-price-point products or services.

Let's go back to our comparison of Target and Bloomingdale's. At Target, a typical pair of ladies' dress shoes might be $20 or $30 while at Bloomingdale's, they can be as much as $1,500. Why? First, there is a measurable difference in quality. The shoes simply aren't made the same; the material, the construction, and the styling are all quite different. The net cost of goods is different. Second, at Bloomingdale's, you receive the personal attention and assistance of the salespeople in selecting the right shoes. The value and expertise required to perform or deliver the product or service are different. Third, the surroundings, the décor of the shoe salon, the product packaging, and the inventory on hand are completely different. The operating expenses for the product are different. Bloomingdale's provides a higher-quality product, a better product selection, and an exclusive client experience, so they can and should charge more. The market value for the two stores is different.

Does this mean Bloomingdale's is a better business than Target? No, Target is equally good at what they do because they too speak directly to their demographic in their value proposition. They too provide all the things their ideal clients want and expect. Both companies have spent time identifying their market, and they cater every message, every presentation, and every experience to these exact clients. Their branding, advertisements, and core values all attract their ideal clients. One is not overcharging or undercharging. Each is doing their thing, in their lane. You need to do it too in order to be profitable. Own your worth. To own your worth, you must know your value, your products, your services, and your ideal clients.

Here is the lesson, loud and clear:

- List what you do for your clients
- List the value it has to them
- Leave your needs and emotions out of your prices
- Focus on your clients' needs
- Provide more value to fewer people
- Price to be profitable
- Swim in your lane

CHAPTER 6

Is It Time to Grow?

When is it time to hire your first employee? For me, it's when I'm working at my desk, doing paperwork, and when it's time to leave for a sales call, I catch myself thinking, "I wish I didn't have this appointment now; I have too much work to do."

Huh? What? I have an opportunity to earn a new client, to make a new sale, and I want to stay at the showroom? Um, hello, earth to LuAnn!

Something is very wrong with this picture. Every time someone calls us, every time someone invites us to sell to them, we need to do exactly that. As the owner of your business, you are its primary advocate. Therefore you are, with near certainty, the best salesperson for your company. Your business will struggle if its best salesperson is in doing paperwork rather than out on a new sales call.

However, it's also important to recognize that when you can't complete tasks and projects in a timely manner, it may affect your reputation with your customers and your vendors. When you are too busy to go out and make more money, it's a pretty good indicator that you need some help.

Other Indicators It Is Time to Hire

Work is affecting your personal life. When you are at the point that you need to hire someone, you are probably struggling at home too. You open the fridge, and you have mayonnaise and mustard staring at you, maybe some wilted lettuce. Or you look in the mirror and think, "Either I get these roots touched up soon, or this gray is my new color!" My friend Edie once said to me, "I remember a period in my business when I was so busy and overwhelmed that I considered putting my kids to bed in their school clothes just so I could get to work earlier." That's stress.

You always experience an unhealthy revenue cycle. A common challenge of solo entrepreneurship is creating a healthy flow of incoming business—keeping the pipeline full, if you will. When you are busy with current projects, marketing and client outreach often go by the wayside. This creates a cycle of busy, slow, busy, slow, which is unhealthy for your business. When the cycle goes up and down solely because you aren't planning and looking ahead, you can't anticipate your revenues, and this makes it very difficult to manage your money. It's also a feast to famine in your checkbook that convinces you that you can't afford to hire.

You need to guard against being so immersed in current projects that you ignore planning for the next one or two quarters. The answer is to have time to manage your entire business, not just the actual tasks of your business. Plan your marketing for the year, so you create leads every week, every month. This allows you to forecast and decide if you need to put people in place to handle the workload and help you create even more business. The goal of a healthy business is to have a consistent pipeline of clients and projects.

Strategy has gone out the window. Another indicator it might be time to hire is you have stopped working *on* your business because you are always working *in* your business. You have a list of new marketing ideas or new tech tools to master, but everything is on a back burner because you are inundated with the everyday tasks of running your business. And worse, you are not dreaming anymore. You are not thinking about new ideas or new products or making time for conferences and classes to energize and inspire you. It's not a waste of time to work on your business. Doing admin work that someone else can do easily and competently is a waste of talent and time. It's important and valuable to create the time for you to strategize and grow your company.

If you're even half as exhausted, stressed, and frustrated as I have described, the next thing you're thinking is, how do I hire someone, and how do I know they are the right person?

First, a Gut Check

We both know you need to get out of this unhealthy, unproductive, unprofitable cycle; however, before moving ahead, be sure to evaluate yourself and your workday. Are you working in an organized and productive way? You're not spending time on Facebook and Instagram when you should be doing your bills, right?

Also, you have identified and documented your systems as we discussed in chapter 3, right? I'll just say this right out: If you haven't set up your systems, don't bother going any further in the hiring process. If you don't have a handle on what you do, when you do it, and why you do it, how can you possibly teach someone to do it? It's a recipe for even more frustration, lost time, and money wasted. Please go back to chapter 3, figure out your systems and document them, and then come back here to find out how to hire.

It's precisely the organized systems that enable you to delegate work to the new hire. The clearer you can express the job description, the responsibilities, and the expectations, the quicker your new hire can jump into the job and get to the business of helping you. At a minimum, you have to have systems, even if you haven't documented them quite yet. Meaning, if you have a set of systems, and you use them yourself and can describe them, then you can at least explain them to a new hire. Ultimately, maybe you even give the new hire the task of documenting the systems, so you have them going forward.

Identify Who You Are Looking For

When you are ready to hire someone, you first need to know who you are looking for and how you will utilize this person. To find out, begin by making a complete list of every job and task required to operate your business every day. Include everything from opening the door to answering the phone, taking the messages off the machine, opening email and snail mail, doing social media posts, ordering inventory, paying the bills, and cleaning the office—every single thing. This is your master list.

From this master list, you will make a second list. It will include the things only you can do. Examples might be, only you can sign checks, meet new clients for signing contracts, determine your yearly budget, set your marketing calendar for the year, and meet with your tax coach. Whatever these are, write them down. Additionally, this list will include the remaining items on your master list that you deeply enjoy doing and you are exceptional at doing. Maybe you are not the only one who can do it, but you really like doing it. Move any of these items over to your second list.

The remaining items on the master list—everything you can't stand doing and everything you aren't very good at doing—make up a third list.

Here are your three lists:

1. Master list of all tasks.
2. List of things only you can do, things you're great at, and things you love doing.
3. List of things you dislike doing, and things you're not good at.

Look very carefully at your last list. This list is the job description for your new hire. These tasks are probably the things you kick around all week and avoid doing until they *must* be done. You are not the best person to do these jobs anyway; they are likely outside of your "genius zone."

Consider what skills and temperament are best to handle the tasks on this list. Do you need an introvert? Do you need an extrovert? You're not hiring a friend here, so leave that off the table. If you are an extrovert and this list suits an introvert, then that's who you are looking for. You already have friends and family. This is an employee.

When I look back at the early years of our business, I see how many of our first hires were unsuccessful because, unknowingly, we naturally hired people who were like us. Like most of us, we gravitate to personalities like ours. My husband and I are both outgoing people, very driven, and intensely goal-orientated. And these are important qualities if you are in your own business where you put everything on the line every day. However, we were usually hiring a person to be our showroom coordinator, a critical position, as this person is the hub of our business. This position coordinates all the activities between salespeople and installers; between customers, salespeople, and installers; and between vendors and us. This position is also responsible for painstakingly checking every invoice for accuracy, as well as ordering and receiving all our product, office supplies, and sample catalogs. It's a massive job, and it requires acute attention to detail and an ability to stay focused for long periods, an ability to coordinate various details over many days and weeks, and an absolute ability to zone in with your head down and get your work done. The best person for this job? Well, after thirty-five years, I can tell you it's not the same person who is best for a sales position. It's not a broad-stroke thinker, it's not someone who doesn't like to be at a desk all day, and it's not someone who thrives on lots of outside stimulus and interaction; it's someone whose personality and skill set are very different from ours. Lesson learned.

In regard to looking for the right person, one lesson I have learned by observing the many employees we have had over the years—as well as my husband, myself, and our kids for that matter—is:

Your Superpower = Your Achilles' Heel.

Don't be surprised when you notice that for most of us, our most dominant traits are the source of both our strengths and our weaknesses. Meaning the exact personality traits that are our superpowers and make us so good and so right for our job can also be the traits that drive those around us nuts or can work against us.

For example, the ideal traits for salespeople include confidence, gregariousness, enthusiasm, and assertiveness. Salespeople are accustomed to taking the lead; we usually seek excitement and new adventures. This works in our favor in most situations, especially in sales presentations. However, sometimes, in small groups, salespeople can come off as bold or brash. We may not allow for others, especially quieter personalities, to have their say. You wouldn't want a salesperson who is timid or uneasy in new surroundings, but at times you need to rein in this personality and caution them not to railroad over peers. You can teach them to dial it back, but it might take beating them over the head several times before they get it. For the record, I may or may not know this from personal experience.

There was a time when I noticed my theory of "Superpower = Achilles' Heel" in our youngest daughter. She was a freshman in high school and was going to spring training in Walt Disney's Wide World of Sports in Florida with her high school softball team. She was and is a highly organized, timely, detail-orientated person who thrives in orderly environments where the rules and expectations are clearly defined and followed. So the new coach held a meeting with all the players and parents two nights before the trip where he laid out the itinerary and the ground rules. It turned out he was strict, direct, and clear. He had expectations of conduct, schedules, and even their travel clothing, meaning no belly shirts, no strappy tank tops, and no sweatpants. They were to look and behave like classy, young women when representing their school.

Well, this was fantastic! You see, my husband and I were just a tad concerned about her traveling with the team since she was only a freshman. Let's face it, when you are twenty-four years old, it's not a big deal spending time with a twenty-eight-year-old, but when you are fourteen years old, there is a huge difference in spending time with eighteen-year-olds. And if it were a loosey-goosey environment, we were concerned she might be overwhelmed on the trip. Not enough to consider for one minute not letting her go, but enough for us to have the concerns. However, after his little talk, which was truthfully more like a drill sergeant at boot camp with a batch of recruits, we knew she would be fine. She loves rules, parameters, and standards. Chaos and disorder are not her friends.

The last thing the coach said to everyone before leaving that night was, "Be at the pre-security area at Newark Airport at 8:00 a.m., sharp. Anyone late will be left behind, no exceptions."

My husband turned to me with a look that said, "Did you hear that? No one can be late." He wasn't worried about our daughter; she was *always* on time. I don't think I woke her up for school, a job, anything since she was in second grade. It was me he was worried about, and he was sending his message to me loud and clear, "Don't make her late, or she will be humiliated in front of the coach and the team."

Duly noted.

So, the morning of the trip, as expected, they were both up bright early, ah, but so was I.

We were out of the house and on our way long before necessary (well before I thought was necessary, but I was keeping my mouth shut). We arrived at the airport, and my husband suggested, even though we had time, he would drop us off and park the car (so she could be even earlier, let's be real). She and I went in, carrying her duffle bag, her bat bag, and her suitcase. At the exact moment we walked in the terminal, I got a sick feeling in my stomach; we were in the wrong terminal. We went to the United terminal out of habit because we would always fly

United, but they were flying American, Delta, or some other airline, and this terminal was United only.

My heart skipped a beat. She hadn't realized it yet. I hesitatingly said to her, "Uh . . . pup . . . we're in the wrong terminal." She turned to me with terror in her eyes. Immediately, I started scrambling for my cell phone to call my husband to come back. I found it; I dialed, he wasn't answering. I dialed; again, he wasn't answering. She looked at me not saying a word, but her face was transparent, "I'm going to be late, I cannot be late. Mom, I cannot be late."

Okay, decision made. I said, "C'mon, let's go."

She fired back at me, "Go where?"

"To the right terminal—we're running there!"

If you could have seen her face!

Okay, maybe you can't understand exactly what this means, but she certainly did. The next terminal is not just out a door, in a door. At Newark, the terminals are situated around a big circle of four and five lanes of intersecting service roads and ramps; there are no sidewalks, no crosswalks—it's not set up for pedestrians. I knew it was a crazy idea, but I also knew my husband probably wouldn't see I had been calling him until he got into the terminal himself and realized the same thing we did, he was in the wrong place. Then, by the time he got back to the parking lot, picked us up, and drove us to the right terminal, she would be dead in the water. Nope, we had to run for it.

She had a few moments of we can't do this, this is impossible, but I was hollering, "Get moving, let's go!"

Out the terminal, we went toward the highway. We were scrambling. She was trying to manage her suitcase, and I was carrying her duffle bag on one shoulder and her bat bag on the other. We were running the highways of the airport. Cars were whizzing by, taxis were jockeying in and out of lanes, and there we were OJ'ing it to the next terminal. It was truly insane! Running ahead of her, I looked back to tell her to step on it, and I could see she was panic-stricken. The look on her face was just nuts! Here were the personality trait differences: Suddenly, I found it hysterical! I'm not off tilt in chaos. I couldn't help but laugh out loud at the two of us. And then I started ribbing her, "It's a race! It's a race! I'm weeening, I'm weening!"

Do you know the movie *Rat Race* with Rowan Atkinson and John Cleese? It's a hilarious ensemble movie about a scavenger hunt race. Every time Rowan Atkinson's character takes the lead, he shouts in this crazy accent, "It's a race, it's a race! I'm weening, I'm weening!"

So I was yelling this to her, laughing my head off at the absurdity of the situation, and she was bordering between crying and laughing, but mostly crying.

Remember, her superpowers are her timeliness, her stability, and her reliability. At this moment, which was genuinely hysterical, she was none of these. She couldn't let go and see the insanity of it; she could only picture the look on the coach's face when she walked in late.

Two sides of an amazing trait. Superpower = Achilles' Heel.

Oh, by the way, we made it, at 7:58 a.m. exactly, I checked. I was extremely pleased; she was much less so.

An important point to consider is, sometimes the first hire isn't someone for your business. Maybe if you hire someone to relieve the "home" duties, you could handle the work duties. If you spend four hours a week cleaning your house, two hours a week grocery shopping, five hours a week making dinner, and five hours a week carpooling, it adds up to sixteen hours a week you are not in your business. It's also a decent part-time job for someone who might be easier to find and train than someone for your business. Think outside the box; there are always solutions.

Find Your New Hire

After you have identified the right personality type and put together the job description for your new hire, next consider, do you need someone full-time or part-time, and does the new hire need to be on site, or could you hire a virtual assistant or a subcontractor? For example, if you need someone to do your bookkeeping, you can hire a service for this rather than take on the salary, benefits, and everything that goes with an employee.

At this point, you need to research how to find the employee you are looking for and how much you should pay this person. Talk with other business owners, colleagues in networking groups, and friends about the salary ranges for this employee. Hopefully, you're a part of organizations in your industry, and you also have your mentor who you can ask for guidance in this area.

When posting a job, whether it's on LinkedIn, Indeed or Monster, realize for an entry-level hire, you probably don't need someone with experience in your direct field. Systems are systems, and though the tasks in your systems are specific to your business or industry, smart, self-directed people will easily transfer their skills from one industry to another.

Set Everyone Up for Success

Be sure to set everyone up for success by training all your new hires thoroughly. Teach them everything they need to know to do their job well. Teach them your systems and make it clear, they are to follow the systems to the letter. It's not okay for you to do things your way and for them to do things their way. It's imperative that every task is done the same way by everyone. This increases productivity, enables crosschecks, and saves time and money. Perhaps your employees will have ideas for improvements to your systems or suggestions for new systems. Many of our best procedures have come from our employees over the years. Changing, revising, and fine-tuning systems is terrific, as long as it's carried out company-wide. If you do determine a new way to do something, revise your procedures manual and consider it a win. The only thing you can't allow is for an employee to operate outside of your systems, to do it "their way." By definition, this is not a system.

To further promote success, I suggest you have weekly meetings with your staff, even if it's only you and one other person. At the weekly meetings, you ensure that your employees' objectives are clear and understood, you create a place and time for deeper questions, and you track how they are performing in their position. Each week, take time to talk about the previous week as well as the week ahead. Talk about the things they are struggling with and brainstorm ways you can help them. It's also important to shine a light on their wins. Take time to notice the positive, reinforce it, and reward it, even if it's with a simple and sincere "High Five!"

Another essential key to your employees' success is to delegate and empower them to do their job. Don't micromanage your people. You have your weekly meetings to evaluate, instruct, and review. The rest of the week, give them the space and the responsibility to do their job. By doing this, you display good leadership, you instill confidence and loyalty, and you create a happy, productive work environment for everyone.

Now, get ready for some magic. When you have your systems in place, and you have found the right person to compliment your skills, your first hire will almost always increase your revenues, which will increase your profits.

CHAPTER 7

Customer Satisfaction, Guaranteed

It Can't Just Be a Sign on the Wall

When it comes to customer service, you have to do what you say you are going to do and then *a little bit more*. Give more, be known for more. When you provide an excellent customer service experience, you create loyal repeat customers and clients. These loyal customers become brand ambassadors for your company. They tell friends, relatives, and social media about you—just like the people in the newcomer's Facebook group were so quick to jump in and sing our praises. Referrals like these result in warm and often hot leads, which are the lifeblood of a profitable business. Loyalty like this is earned by providing an outstanding experience with your company. Create a company that people want to do business with and are proud enough of to refer others to you.

I explained in the first chapter how I was influenced by the example of my father-in-law as an exceptional businessperson, and that's true, but I also have a drive to do my best in everything I do. I love the saying, which I have on my vision board, "The way you do anything is the way you do everything." It speaks to me—it inspires me.

As I mentioned before, our daughters played softball. They both played competitive travel softball from middle school through college, and the games and tournaments were family events. My husband often coached the girls' teams, and every spring and summer weekend, we traveled together throughout the mid-Atlantic region for all of the games. Although I didn't coach these teams, I loved being there, and I even kept my own stat book every year. One time during a game, as I was cheering the girls on, shouting something or other from the sidelines, a player sitting next to my daughter glanced over at me. We shared a quick smile, and then she turned to my daughter and said something. They looked at me, looked back at each other, and then giggled.

Later, when we were eating dinner, I asked my daughter, "By the way, what did Monica say to you earlier today?"

"Oh," my daughter replied, "she said, 'Your mom is so into this. I mean she keeps her own book, she pays attention to every play instead of sitting with the other moms . . . what's up with that? Did she play college softball or something?'"

"What did you say? You were both giggling; what was so funny?"

"I just told her, 'That's you. That my mom does crazy, full tilt, 110 percent with everything, all the time.'"

How to Provide Excellent Customer Service

Here are the ways to bring 110 percent to the customer service experience.

Lead by example. It begins with you and your genuine desire as the leader of your company to make every customer thrilled to do business with you. You know you must exhibit this to your customers, but it's also extremely important to exhibit this to your employees. When you go the extra mile, when you give 110 percent, your employees notice and understand "This is how we do things here"—just the way my daughter noticed, "That's just how my mom is."

You should have conversations, lots of conversations with your staff about the ways all of you can serve your clients and make their experience with your company remarkable. If your employees are on the front line with your clients, whether it's face to face or on the phone, speak with them and ask if they have insights and creative ideas of how to offer more value to your clients. Take the time to discuss this and to encourage your team always to look for ways to show appreciation to your customers.

Your team chemistry is critical. The most successful teams like each other. They like being together, they like and appreciate each other's personalities, and they laugh easily with one another. This is true whether we are referring to sports teams, rock bands or businesses. Successful teams have respect for each other, value each other's skill sets, and enjoy each other's company and because of this, they perform better. You have heard the saying: "Happy wife, happy life." While I do particularly like that adage myself, I happen to like this one just as much: "Happy company, happy customers." A team that feels valued and appreciated brings this sentiment to your customers. When your employees have pride in the company, your clients will notice this and admire it.

Vendors and suppliers are part of your team as well. It's imperative that the resources you rely on share the same 110 percent philosophy as you. Always ask about a vendor's customer service and satisfaction policies before setting up an account. Truthfully, though, more essential than their policies are their values. Policies are "what the book says"; values are where the real customer service lives. You need vendors who give you exactly what you give your clients. The absolute basics include: to be heard, to be treated fairly, to be understood, and to receive quality products and services in a timely manner. Your clients don't want a talking head, and neither do you. For you to provide this to your customers, your vendors *must* have the same outlook. To find out which vendors and companies provide real customer service and not lip service, you should speak with colleagues who already use their services.

Ask probing questions such as:

- How would you handle a situation where you received the wrong item even though you ordered it correctly?
- What would you do if you ordered the wrong item?
- What happens when you have a technical problem and you require more help than what a phone call can resolve?
- If you need pricing outside of standard specifications, how do you get it?
- What happens when you receive damaged goods?
- What is the typical response time to phone calls and emails?

Questions like these will help you determine how sensitive a vendor is to your satisfaction regardless of what their policy book is.

Listen, really, truly listen. Listening is without question one of the most valuable skills you can cultivate not only to provide unparalleled customer service but also to run a successful business. But to be clear, I mean active, intentional listening. If you are like most people, you probably consider yourself a good listener. Take a moment and recall a recent meeting with prospective clients. What did you learn about them? If you were listening more than talking, you should know a decent amount of information about them, their needs, and their personal lives.

It's one thing to learn the surface information such as:

- How did they hear about you?
- Are they married?
- Do they have kids?
- How long have they lived in their home?
- What do they do for a living?

The above are examples of basic details you should have learned. But are you picking up the more significant details—the things people don't say point blank but infer through the stories they tell or the reactions they have or by their opinions on events in the media? These are the details that will help you provide outstanding customer service.

- Are they action takers?
- Are they impulsive?
- Are they active, intentional listeners?
- Do they mull over and consider decisions?
- Are they likely to confer with someone before deciding on big purchases?
- Do they already have other quotes or appointments for more estimates?
- Are they easily influenced by what friends or family members think?
- Are they comfortable speaking up for themselves, or do they find this difficult?
- Are they interested in the details, or are they big-picture people?
- Do they have previous experience with your types of products or services?

When you pay attention and listen intentionally, you will find that your customers are telling you exactly how to satisfy them and make them happy. Take cues from their conversations to understand their personality and what matters to them. With this information, you can provide the exact ways to delight and impress them as individuals.

Think about it; it's similar to how you pay attention to your spouse or kids when it's time to get a gift for them. You would never purchase anything random, something unrelated to them as a person, and then expect it to be especially noticed or appreciated. No, if you want them to feel appreciated and delighted, you pay attention to what they like, what they respond to, and you select something just for them.

Excellent customer service is exactly the same. Pay attention, listen, and look for the clues—the unsaid cues. One person will value quick delivery; another will value many choices while another will be frustrated by too much advice or suggestions. Some people will need to see pictures; others will want data and research. Listen and discover what resonates with each individual. When you deliver on that, you will create a powerful relationship with your clients. This instills loyalty for your company and your brand, and it creates brand ambassadors.

To cultivate your listening skills, here is a little exercise you can play with: Practice not speaking until your clients have fully completed their sentences. This is not as easy as you might think. You can't interrupt, you can't finish their sentences, you can't agree and then talk over them, and you can't jump in with your own example or story. You can't say a word until they have completely stopped talking. It's challenging, but it's worthwhile doing. The gems you learn are so valuable!

If you really want to sharpen your listening skills, try starting every sentence you say with a word that begins with the same letter of the last word they said. This is hard and takes great concentration, but if you can do this, you are truly, intentionally listening.

Listening skills are imperative for productive relationships with your clients. I have also found that this skill has helped me tremendously in my podcast. People are so happy when they feel they have been heard and understood. We are all this way; it's natural to crave and enjoy this. After being interviewed, many of my guests compliment me on my interviewing skills and technique. My guests appreciate the questions I ask and that I probe for more information. Because I practice not interrupting them, they are given the space to fully develop their concepts and thoughts for my listeners. They express being impressed with me, but I know I'm simply listening intentionally, which is something everyone likes. Because few people listen with intention, when you do it is noticed. Your clients will notice it too. The best part is, both of you will benefit from it.

Intentional listening applies whether you are in the process of making a sale, in the process of delivering your product or service, or in the stressful process of handling an unsatisfied customer. Listening is paramount to have a good outcome when clients are unhappy with your product or service. The answer is always in the listening. Your clients will always share some nugget of information that will help you provide them with what they want in order to be happy.

The Results of an Excellent Customer Service Process

Increased gross sales. The simple truth is with very few exceptions, people are willing to pay more when they receive more, and that includes having a better customer service experience. Like you, your clients are busy, and they want to do business with people who make the process better for them, with people who make the process "about them."

According to a Salesforce article, "86% of buyers will pay more for a better customer experience. But only 1% of customers feel that vendors consistently meet their expectations."[10]

Be part of the 86%.

That may mean, like us at Window Works, you make appointments in the evening, or you have a free shop-at-home service. These are just two examples of how we serve our customers, making life and making doing business with us easier for them. Take a moment and think outside the box. Do some brainstorming. What could you do for your clients to make their time with your company more satisfying? How could you make the process less stressful for them? What are the things you could do that your competition is not doing? Look there.

Increased net profit margins. We all know it's important to sell more; however, it's equally important to keep more, to strive for higher

---

10 Hanington, J. (2014, April 7). 9 Must-Know Stats for the Customer-Centric Marketer [Web log post]. Retrieved November 29, 2017, from https://www.pardot.com/blog/9-must-know-stats-customer-centric-marketer/

net profits. Having higher net profits is like hitting the gym each week or going to your yoga class and building a healthy base that sustains you through illness or injury. You need a healthy net profit for down times, for growth, for capital improvements, and for salary distribution. Customer service factors into your net profits because we all know it costs a business much more money to attract new clients than it does to sell again to existing clients. Money spent on advertising and time spent on developing social media campaigns and various other marketing initiatives to find new clients eat into your net profits. However, you only get the opportunity to sell again to existing clients when you treat them well and provide value and top-notch customer service.

A stellar reputation. The good news is, how your company performs and executes on its promises spreads through your community, virtual or otherwise, like wildfire. The bad news is, how your company performs and executes on its promises spreads through your community, virtual or otherwise, like wildfire. Funny, but not funny. Particularly in this age of social media, it's more important than ever to be diligent in every transaction with every client.

Decide to be the company known for exceptional customer service and let that spread like wildfire. Be the company people talk well about and write great reviews of, the company people return to because they know what they are getting and they like it. Do the right thing by your clients; treat them how you would like to be treated. When you work hard with the intention to create a stellar reputation through exceptional customer service, you will be rewarded tenfold with repeat business and referrals.

CHAPTER 8

Be Prepared so You Can Be "Lucky"

Hopefully one day, many years from now, friends, family, and clients will look at the business you have created and say to you, "Boy, you sure are lucky! You're so successful. I guess you are just one of those people!" When this happens, you will think to yourself, are they out of their mind? Lucky? Yup, lucky enough to work through weekends, to work through family vacations, to regularly pull fourteen-hour days. Yup, I'm lucky all right! Well, instead of snapping at your friend, just smile and say, "Yes, I have been very fortunate, and I am grateful for my booming business." *Then think of me at the exact moment* and know that I know you have not been lucky. I know if you have become one of the rare business owners who survive many years and can count these as successful years, it's because you have worked hard and you constantly have prepared so you could be "Lucky."

How do you "prepare to be lucky"?

Be the Expert

To be lucky, you must commit to getting better every day at your profession. It doesn't happen by accident; it happens through intention and action. We all have that friend who is in great shape, never seems to diet or talk about missing her favorite dishes, and never seems to be fighting herself over food. At dinners out, she has what you have—a salad, dinner, wine, and dessert. How does she do that? Oh, it's her metabolism; she's just lucky. Maybe, but more likely not. Ask her; I'll bet you find she is exercising and eating clean all week—not having three-course meals with dessert every night. She actively commits to her exercise and food regimen day in and day out so she can be the lucky person who can "eat whatever she wants."

Business is the same way. To be an expert both in your industry and in business, you must actively commit to it. Just like our girlfriend who blocks time for her workouts, actively block time to learn the skills and information you need to be the best you can be.

Here are some things you can do to be the expert:

- Read books, respected blogs, and trade publications.
- Listen to audiobooks and podcasts.
- Join industry and trade organizations.
- Attend conferences within your industry.
- Attend conferences outside your industry on topics such as marketing, technology, and personal development.
- Join masterminds, again both inside and outside your specific industry.

You can certainly become more knowledgeable year by year in the course of running your business by randomly doing the above suggestions throughout your career.

But if you want to cut to the chase, up your game, and become the expert quicker, you could set up a calendar of topics for the coming year.

Each month, you dive deep into a particular area, read up on it, attend a conference, listen to audiobooks or podcasts, and watch webinars. There are dozens of ways to learn. Pick the way that works for you.

Address these three areas:

- Industry information
- Business management and operation
- Tech tools
- Take some time to brainstorm. Be honest with yourself.
- In what areas are you lacking knowledge, skills, or both?
- In what areas do you have enough talent to be dangerous but not enough to be effective?
- What topics really interest you, and what would you enjoy learning more about?

Make a page for each month. List the month, the topic, and the action items you can take to achieve mastery.

Month: _____ Topic_____

Actions:

- _____
- _____
- _____
- _____

Here is a three-month example that mixes business skills, industry skills, and tech skills.

January: Business Skills: Bookkeeping and Tax Prep

- Meet with my accountant and commit to understanding what she needs every month during the year, why she needs it, how to track it, and how to provide it to her efficiently. Ask her to teach me how to evaluate the financial health of my business.

- Investigate software like QuickBooks or FreshBooks. Read up and speak with my accountant and colleagues to find out how a tool like this can increase the efficiency and accuracy of my invoicing and record keeping.
- Review my vendor accounts and ensure I have negotiated the best pricing. Also, ask if they have a promo schedule for the year ahead and make a plan to incorporate it into my marketing.

February: Product Knowledge: Drapery Hardware

- One hour per week, read and understand all the features of a particular line. Learn all of the options related to the line: rod diameter, bracket options, colors, traversing options, finial styles, ring styles, delivery times, and price points. Know the line inside and out.

March: Tech Tools: Social Media Marketing

- Investigate advertising on Facebook, Instagram, LinkedIn, Pinterest, or Twitter. Find out where our target customers spend their time. Decide which platform is the very best place for us to spend our time and money on.
- Each week, spend one hour learning how the platform works, how much it costs, and what constitutes a good ad or campaign.
- By the end of the month, put in place a three-month campaign for this platform. Schedule an evaluation of the results at the completion.
- Decide to repeat, discontinue, or learn another social media platform for the next campaign.

Research Your Competition

Spend time researching your competition. Be respectful of their time, of course, but call them and listen to how they answer the phone and handle a new inquiry. Ask questions related to the products or services; ask how they charge and what is included. If you can secret shop them, again being respectful of their time, I'm all for it.

Do an honest comparison. By doing some comparing, you will learn what you like about your own company and what you want to continue. You will also get ideas on how you can improve. Do you measure up? Could you do more for your clients?

Knowing about your competition, their strengths and their weaknesses, is helpful when potential clients have other estimates. When you know your competition well, you can position your presentation to highlight the features where you outperform them. For instance, we are one of very few custom window treatment retailers in our area that still offer free measuring and free installation. This sets us apart, and we talk about it often. We explain in our introductory phone call with potential clients that they have no risk and no obligation when meeting with us for ideas and designs.

Recently, a previous client of ours called our showroom to make a new appointment for wood blinds. As she was making the appointment, she said to my showroom coordinator, "Please tell LuAnn I want to do business with her, but she needs to know XYZ Store is offering 25 percent off Hunter Douglas wood blinds this month."

Okay, I knew this store charged for both the measuring and the installation, so we made a little comparison before I went over to the client. Here is what we learned. Yes, the other store was legitimately giving 25 percent off the blinds. But when we added their per-room measuring fee and their per-blind installation fee, the exact same four wood blinds for two bedrooms with no discount from us were a total of $165 more through XYZ Store. When I met with the client, she asked me if I would match the price of the other store since they were giving 25 percent off. I very happily explained to her that yes, I would charge her $165 more than I had intended but thought she might rather have the Window Works price before competitor matching! We had a nice laugh over that, and she ordered the blinds from us.

Know your competition, know what they do and don't offer, and definitely know how you differ from them.

When you decide to be an expert in addition to increasing confidence in yourself, your clients will experience tremendous confidence in you as well. This translates to more sales. People want to know they are in good hands when they spend their money.

I don't remember who it was, but I do remember someone once said to my husband, "Everything you touch turns to gold." We know it looks like we are lucky, but we know how hard we work every day. Don't misunderstand me; we enjoy it, and we are not complaining, never. It's important to us, so we decide to do what it takes. This is my point: If you want above average success, it's not going to happen by luck; you have to do the work. If it's important to you too, challenge yourself to do the same thing in your business.

CHAPTER 9

Design Your Dream Business

Dream, Visualize, Intend

In the previous chapters, we discussed the tangible, actionable steps for running your business. Those chapters provide you with a realistic, step-by-step roadmap for success. This chapter is about dreaming, disconnecting from the logical, and about cultivating your inner voice and intuition. You must make time to wonder what the possibilities are for you and your business. For incredible things to happen, you have to visualize and intend bigger ideas than you ever thought possible or logical.

Six months after my husband and I had bought our first house, I started thinking about how I would change it if I could. Don't misunderstand me; I loved that house. It was beautiful, and it was much more than I had ever thought my first home would be. However, I always think ahead. What will be next? I know for a fact this doesn't come from being unhappy where I am; it comes from the opposite place. I feel so grateful to have what I have, or for an opportunity I get, that I automatically start building on it and dreaming about what else is possible. So after a hot minute in my dream house, I began dreaming about how to change it. Logical, right?

One day, I wrote a list of all the features I would have in my perfect dream house, whether they made sense for my ranch house or not. I didn't know if we would eventually renovate this house or what. I didn't care. I just made a list of all the things I wanted most in a home. There were some twenty-five items on this list.

Here are some of them:

- Center hall colonial.
- Beautiful foyer entrance with a staircase.
- A back staircase. Now, that's a bit crazy. How many houses have two staircases anyway, I mean ones that aren't on Downton Abbey?
- Big, bay-shaped kitchen eating area.
- The house will sit at the end of a round cul-de-sac, not on the side leading to the end, at the very end.

After I had made the list, I tucked it in a book. I just put it out to the universe. How I could have two staircases or a center hall colonial when my house was a ranch was not something I worried about; I let the universe worry about that.

Thirteen years later, we decided to move. We bought a new construction home that was already underway. The architect's plans were done, and the foundation was in. The builder said if we hired an architect, we could change anything we wanted other than the footprint. Not wanting this expense, we looked at his plan and went ahead with the original home, which was a beautiful design.

A couple of months after we had moved in, I was setting up my bookshelves. I came across the book with my "dream house" list. Looking at the list for the first time in thirteen years, I was stunned to see nearly every single thing on my list was in this house. In fact, there were only two things on the list missing in the house! Our new house had an open-plan kitchen with a bay window in the eating area, it had a fireplace in the family room, and it was the very last house on a cul-de-sac. It even had a front and a back staircase!

I ran downstairs and showed the list to my husband. We sat there stunned. I hadn't designed the architecture of this house. During the entire process of building this house, I hadn't even remembered I had made my dream house list. The level of details and the kind of details on my dream house list that were in this house were insane.

When my husband noticed the two missing details, he said to me, "Well, Lu, I can't put a fireplace in our master bedroom, but I certainly can build a front porch on this house for you!"

I thanked him and said, "Not necessary; twenty-three out of twenty-five features is just perfect for me!"

Let the Universe Know What You Want

The universe listens, so put out there what you want for your business. Make a list of all that you want to accomplish—all the wonderful things you will create and all the ways you will serve your clients.

Dreaming and setting goals for yourself and your business is best done where your imagination can run unchecked. To discover where you do this type of thinking, pay attention to what you are doing when your mind roams. Does your mind roam when you exercise, read, go for a long drive, meditate, or sit quietly?

If this is new for you, once you have discovered where your imagination unleashes, make a point to do this several times a month, with intention. Take notice: What would your business look like if you had a magic wand?

- Do you stay solo, working when and how you want without the pressure of staff?
- Do you have three employees or fifty employees?

- Are you well-known in your community, on the mayor's speed dial?
- Do you get quoted in *Inc. Magazine*?
- Do you have locations all over the state, the country, the world?

This exercise isn't just about the goals that seem reachable; include everything you would like to achieve, even if it seems unattainable. Do you want a front and a back staircase? Your list is based on your dreams, not reality, not logic.

You can do this with an actual vision board. I do my vision boards old school style. I scour magazines for weeks, clipping pictures, words, and snippets of copy that speak to me, that represent my wildest dreams. Then I arrange all the pictures on a big, tri-panel, heavy-duty poster board, which I put in front of me at my desk. The last time I made one, I even had it made a real framed canvas through canvasart.com. That's commitment, I'm just sayin.

Do you want to know some of the things on my vision board? I have a picture of a woman surfing a big wave because I want to do that. Mind you, I haven't learned to surf yet, and I won't tell you how old I am, but still, don't be surprised if you see me on Facebook or Instagram posting a picture one day. I also have pictures of what retirement looks like for Vin and me—bicycling together, walking on beaches, and touring European wine countries. Another picture I have is one of that gorgeous, famous hotel in Dubai with the pool on the balcony. You know the one. I want to be invited to speak in Dubai with travel, speaking fees, and accommodations taken care of, staying in that amazing hotel with Vin. Why? No idea. I keep getting the vision of me doing that, so I put it on my board.

In addition to visualizing your future business, you need to make sure the universe knows you are serious about it. You do this through your actions. For example, I exercise regularly because I know when life slows down, I need to stay strong and athletic so I can surf and cycle the world.

There was a time when we desperately needed to hire an assistant for me. I had never had a direct assistant before. I had our showroom coordinator, but she supported all of us, and I was swamped. I was conducting interviews, but I couldn't find the right fit with the right skillset. The people I interviewed either wanted too many hours or not enough hours or didn't have the skills. This went on for four months. Then I got so busy I couldn't even think about it and put it on the side burner. Soon, though, I set about looking again, but I remained out of luck.

Then one day, I looked around the office and realized we didn't have a space for a new employee to work. We had an extra side counter that random people would sit at to make a note or whatnot but no place for a dedicated five-day-a-week employee. I explained to my husband that we needed to make room and buy a computer for this area. His reply was, "When you find someone, we'll take on that expense."

I begged him, "The universe needs to know we're serious; we have to make room."

We knocked out and moved walls in the office and upended fourteen different things to make room for the extra desk. When all of that was settled, our brand new, perfect employee walked through the door. That's how the universe works.

You get it? No logic, just dreams. The universe wants you to achieve your dreams.

Cultivate Your Inner Voice

By the time I was eighteen years old, I had already moved out of my parents' house. I was living in an apartment and had a job as an exercise instructor at a health club called Figure Magic. This was back in the '80s when Jane Fonda, leg warmers, and leotards were all the rage. Pretty quickly, I made an impression on the managers of the club because I was fearless in selling memberships.

After six months, the manager and the assistant manager sat me down and told me about a new opportunity. They explained a second location was opening soon, and, although they had never promoted someone so young before, they wondered if I would move to the new location and take the position of assistant manager.

It took everything I had not to do a happy dance right there in the office. I am, as my kids now joke with me, a classic overachiever. Here I was, six months into this job, and I was already offered a promotion! My new salary would be $280 a week, $60 more a week than I was currently making! Of course, I thought it was a jackpot, and in my defense, comparatively speaking, it was a huge raise. The place was to open in three months. I was thrilled!

As I rode my bike home from work that night, my mind was racing. I imagined how proud my boyfriend and my parents would be. I started to dream and plan the next step. I still do this, by the way; as soon as a window of opportunity opens, I not only visualize it and what it means for us but also immediately start going down the road of all the things that could come of it. My husband usually looks at me and says something like, "Can we get this done first before you start scheming about the next part?" So I was pedaling along, dreaming about where this would take me. I played it out. How soon could I become the youngest manager of a Figure Magic Salon? Wouldn't that be amazing? First the youngest assistant manager and then the youngest manager? What will it be like to be responsible for the club and the members? I'll be invited to strategy meetings. I'll be involved in training. Oh yes, this is amazing!

Ah, uh oh, hang on a minute, earth to LuAnn! Once I'm the manager, what's next? The only person above the manager is the owner. And what does a manager earn anyway, another $60 per week?

By the fourth mile, instead of being pleased with myself, I was completely disappointed in myself. I thought, you're rationalizing that this is a good thing. You're convincing yourself that because you got noticed, you're some kind of a rock star. But where will you be in a year from now, Miss Big Wig? And how about in three years? Is teaching aerobics classes your big life's dream? *What the heck are you doing with your life, LuAnn?*

You see, I had gone to college the previous fall, and despite being president of my class, an A student, a National Honor Society member, and your basic all-around overachiever, I couldn't hack it. Nope, I dropped out after one semester. Ugh. I just didn't lock it down and do the work. And now I was close to fooling myself that I was "on a career path" because I wanted it to be real and didn't want to face the fact that I may have seriously screwed up my life by not going to college. I was rationalizing big time.

The way I saw it, I had two options. I could take the job and hope I might parlay it into some kind of grand exercising instructor future, or I could do what I did: I walked in the next day, and I quit. I said, "Thank you so much. I appreciate you seeing whatever you see in me to promote me, but that's exactly why I have to leave." I knew in my gut I had to walk away. I was scared and not at all sure what I would do, especially for money, but I knew I had to make moves, and it wasn't down the road to another exercise studio.

Not long ago I had the distinct honor of interviewing Mr. Lee Cockerell for my podcast. Lee is a former executive vice president of operations at Walt Disney World and author of several books including *Creating Disney Magic.* Something he said to me took me back to this very moment in my life. He said, "When you do the hard things, everything else gets easier, but if you only do the easy things, everything else gets harder."

I know there have been many times, starting with that moment when I was eighteen, that I have chosen the hard thing over the easy thing. There is a voice inside of me that speaks to me. She encourages me to be better, and she is real with me. She will never tell me I'm doing the right thing if I'm not. I call her the goddess. You have one too. Your voice always knows what's best for you. The trick is to listen. You can ignore it and drown it out, for sure. Especially when you prefer to do the easy thing over the hard thing, oh yes, you can push that voice down. But why would you? You only trade the hard thing at the moment for the hard thing later. Believe me, I was very tempted to ignore my goddess that day. I was pleading with her like crazy: I could work there for a year, it would be good on my resume, I would gain valuable experience—I had reasons galore. But she persisted. I knew I would get sucked in. I knew my earning potential would top out. I would never reach my life's dreams and goals in that job. As much as I wanted to be the "youngest assistant manager ever," I walked away from the safety of the promotion and bet on myself. I had to do the hard thing and take a risk, just like my goddess said. This applies to life as well as business—and it always pays off.

Be Prepared to Take Risks

You are the designer of your life and your business. If you are not reaching your full potential, what are you doing? What's the point? Staying still is not an option; either you go forward, or you go backward.

In the process of creating a profitable business that you're proud of, you will sometimes trade safety for risk. If you never feel afraid, if you never wonder if you're doing the right thing in your business, then you are playing it too safe. Remember that pivots are okay. Quitting on something is okay. Wrong turns are okay. Restructuring is okay. But standing still is not okay. You get nowhere when you stand still. It's hard to achieve real growth while staying completely safe. Smartly prepare, evaluate, and plan, but ultimately, you will risk something at some point.

Develop a Mantra

I strongly encourage you to develop a mantra to move you either to action or to stillness. You will need both over the course of your business career. The mantra could be anything. You can make it up yourself or copy it from somebody else. There are books out there on the topic that you can read for inspiration. Where it comes from doesn't matter; what matters is that it resonates with you and doesn't let you off the hook.

There are two mantras I've had for many years. The first one is "All I need is within me now," which is from Tony Robbins. He suggests that you say it in a four-part cadence, so you actually say it as a mantra. This mantra moves me to action. When I am apprehensive and ask myself if I can do something or if I made the right decision, I just say to myself, "All I need is within me now." When I first started using this mantra in stressful periods, I would have to say it all day long, throughout the day. Now I can just say it once, and I can feel myself thinking, okay, you got this, move on. You have successes behind you. You'll have successes in front of you. My second mantra is "I will persist until I succeed." This one is by Og Mandino, from *The Greatest Salesman in the World.* I use it when I'm tired and wondering if it's worth it, when I'm feeling overwhelmed, or when something didn't go well. Maybe it was a big something that didn't go well. Then I say, "I will persist until I succeed" because that is who I am, and that is what I do. I've had this mantra since I was ten years old. I have become that person through the mantra and my actions. Whenever I face something that seems too hard, too daunting, too overwhelming, I just say, "I will persist until I succeed." I pick myself up, put my big girl panties on, and do it.

Please find a time, space, and place where you can dream about your business, your goals, and your life. Schedule time for working on your business, not just in your business. If you have the courage, create a vision board. Find a mantra that speaks to you. Write it down. Learn it. Repeat it often.

CHAPTER 10

Practice Acknowledgement and Gratitude

I have discussed everything from creating systems for managing your employees and clients to finding your clients and marketing to them and showing you the power of intuition and visualization. However, my real reason for writing this book is to encourage you to create a business you will be proud of. I want you to know that all the hours, all the missed vacation days, all the difficult times, and all the sleepless nights are worth it. The experience, the gift of having Window Works with my husband Vin and our cousin Bill has been and continues to be priceless.

But the cold fact is, as you know, I was never supposed to have a window treatment company. Growing up, I wasn't interested in decorating, moving around furniture, and dressing dollhouses with curtains and draperies. I had no interest in the interior design industry. As I told you back at the beginning of the book, I was supposed to be president of the United States. I was supposed to go to West Point; from there, I would go into the service where I would have many years as a distinguished officer; then I would be tapped to be senator of my state (clearly because I had been such exemplary officer); and then eventually, naturally, I would be president of the United States.

Um, okay, LuAnn.

You have these ideas as a child, and then you become a young adult, and you realize you don't have the means to actualize them. You don't have the background. You don't have the connections. You don't have anything required to make them a reality. If you are a high achiever and competitive person like me, with big dreams, you say to yourself, "Okay, so maybe I'm not the president of the United States, but I'll be something really fabulous one day." You start to work and the next thing you know, ten years have gone by and reality is knocking at your door.

It was exactly at the ten-year point in our business when I looked around and thought I hadn't accomplished anything with my life. I sold myself out. Where were all my big dreams? I was selling drapes and blinds. I was disappointed in myself and thought, well, what's my next chapter? I was in my early thirties now, and it was high time I got started becoming fabulous.

However, I soon learned, we had what my husband calls the golden handcuffs. He explained to me the business was profitable, but if I left, it would be in jeopardy. During that period in our business, I was responsible for the lion's share of the sales. He explained to me that our family, our employees, and the families of our employees all depended on the income from this business. There would be no jumping ship. My husband quite literally looked at me and said, "It would be selfish of you to leave when so many depend on us."

He was right, so very right.

He usually is by the way.

The years passed by, and one day I found myself in a conversation with a customer who had called on us yet again for more window treatments. Like I always do, I thanked her for remembering us, and she burst into, "Of course I called you again. I would never even consider calling another company!" She began citing the reasons she would call on us, and as she spoke, I heard in her words what we had accomplished. I understood what we had built and what it meant to the people in our community. For the first time, I really heard the reasons people told their family and friends about us. Instead of thinking of it just as polite words, something that people say, I knew it was real. Our customers appreciated our integrity, our work ethic, our expertise, and that we always do our best for them.

From that moment on, I began to see and hear it from numerous customers. It was like someone turned on the lights. I realized it was pretty powerful how we had created a business that not only had survived over twenty years but also was vibrant, valued, and respected. My appreciation for our customers grew exponentially with this knowledge. We were in this together. We get to do these things for them because they rely on us to do it.

Soon I understood I had lived up to my goals and dreams for myself. I knew that I, just like Vin and Bill, had worked my ass off for the last twenty years, and it amounted to something worthwhile, something significant.

Together, we did this.

Together, we earned this.

Together, we had become fabulous.

Take time every day to acknowledge your wins and feel grateful for your business, yourself, your team, and your customers. Don't underestimate what you do. It's meaningful. You are important to your clients and community. Yes, maybe you sometimes work twelve- or fourteen-hour days, but it's your choice to do that. If you need to be reminded why your business is a gift, recall the last job you hated. Stay firmly connected to the feeling of gratefulness. Learn to acknowledge the many ways your business touches and influences other people's lives.

Serve your clients well and do your very best by them, and you will be rewarded with loyalty.

It has already been fifteen years since my "aha" moment, and I can say without reservation, having been part of building and running a successful business continues to be a great satisfaction in my life. The gratitude I have for it is indescribable. Thankfully, I have discovered that being someone fabulous isn't limited to being the president of the United States.

I'm proud of us.

I want you to be proud of you.

Start today.

Create something you will be grateful for many years from now. Go back to the beginning of the book and work your way through it. Set out your mission, put your systems in place, gather your dream team, and identify your ideal client. Make the hard choices and stand by them. Know your reputation is worthwhile and honor it.

Decide to be Excellent.

Made in the USA
San Bernardino, CA
27 April 2019